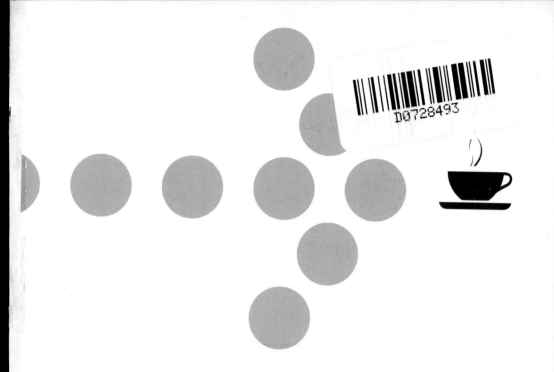

---> **1,000**

---> **RESTAURANT BAR & CAFÉ GRAPHICS**

LUKE HERRIOTT

---> From Signage to Logos and Everything in Between

ROCKPORT

BEVERLY MASSACHUSETTS

···⟩

First published in the United States of America by Rockport Publishers, a member of Quayside Publishing Group

100 Cummings Center

Suite 406-L

Beverly, Massachusetts 01915

Telephone: (978) 282-9590, Fax: (978) 283-2742

www.rockpub.com

ISBN-13: 978-1-59253-550-7

ISBN-10: 1-59253-550-X

···⟩

10 9 8 7 6 5 4 3

Design: Megan Cooney (adapted from 1,000 **Restaurant Bar & Café Graphics** designed by Luke Herriott

Cover Design: Luke Herriott

Printed in China

ROCKPORT

PUBLISHERS

1,000

RESTAURANT BAR & CAFÉ GRAPHICS

From
Signage
to Logos
and Everything
in Between

LUKE HERRIOTT

⋯➔

INTRODUCTION

The restaurant business is a risky and competitive world, and successful design is an essential component in an establishment's survival. A brand that has been cleverly designed portrays the style of a restaurant, bar, or café, helping to draw vital customers in. The work shown in **1,000 Restaurant, Bar, and Café Graphics** demonstrates how to create a concept that will direct and inform subtly and effectively.

A restaurant brand can suggest anything from a luxury dining experience to a cheap, cheerful snack. Successful branding influences who will enter, what they will order, how long they will stay, how much money they will part with, and most important, whether they will be a repeat customer.

This book is a feast of design concepts, showcasing 1,000 fresh ideas from some of the world's most successful and well-known designers. Featuring an international range of eating and drinking establishments, this book explores how brand identity can work its way into every aspect of a business, from its walls, door signs, and window graphics right down to its napkins, matchbooks, and tags.

Be informed and be inspired by what you see—and be sure to give your next project an extra bit of spice.

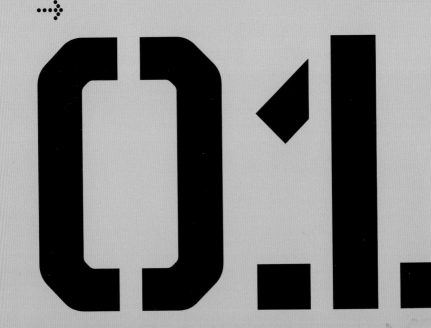

0001—01.74

···▸

CHAPTER 1.
SIGNAGE

EXTERIOR SIGNS
INTERIOR SIGNS
DIRECTIONAL SIGNS
WINDOW GRAPHICS
WALL GRAPHICS

0001 ⇢ Sea Design
⇢ UK

0002 ⇢ Sea Design
⇢ UK

0003 ⇢ Sea Design
⇢ UK

0004 ⇢ i_d buero
⇢ Germany

0005 ⇢ i_d buero
⇢ Germany

0006 ⟶ Studio Output
⟶ UK

0007 ⟶ Studio Output
⟶ UK

0008 ⟶ Studio Output
⟶ UK

0009 ⟶ Studio Output
⟶ UK

0012 ···➤ Willoughby Design Group
    ···➤ USA

0013 ···➤ Willoughby Design Group
    ···➤ USA

0014 ···➤ Willoughby Design Group
    ···➤ USA

0015 ···➤ Willoughby Design Group
    ···➤ USA

0016 ⋯⋗ Willoughby Design Group
⋯⋗ USA

0017 ⋯⋗ Rome & Gold Creative
⋯⋗ USA

0018 ⋯⋗ Rome & Gold Creative
⋯⋗ USA

0019 ⋯⋗ Rome & Gold Creative
⋯⋗ USA

0021 ⇢ Rome & Gold Creative
⇢ USA

0022 ⇢ Rome & Gold Creative
⇢ USA

0023 ⇢ Rome & Gold Creative
⇢ USA

0024 ⇢ Rome & Gold Creative
⇢ USA

0026 ⇢ Mimolimit
⇢ Czech Republic

0027 ⟶ Milton Glaser, Inc
⟶ USA

0028 ⟶ Milton Glaser, Inc
⟶ USA

0029 ⟶ Milton Glaser, Inc
⟶ USA

0030 ⟶ Milton Glaser, Inc
⟶ USA

0031 ⟶ Damion Hickman Design
⟶ USA

0033 ⋯⇥ Hornall Anderson Design Works
⋯⇥ USA

0034 ⋯⇥ Hornall Anderson Design Works
⋯⇥ USA

0035 ⋯⇥ Hornall Anderson Design Works
⋯⇥ USA

0036 ⋯⇥ Hornall Anderson Design Works
⋯⇥ USA

0037 ---> Hornall Anderson Design Works
---> USA

0038 ---> Hornall Anderson Design Works
---> USA

0039 ---> Studio Output
---> UK

0040 ---> Elephant Design Pvt Ltd
---> India

0041 ⋯⇥ **sky design**
⋯⇥ USA

0042 ⋯→ sky design
⋯→ USA

0043 ⋯→ Greiner Design Associates
⋯→ USA

0044 ⋯→ R&Mag Graphic Design
⋯→ Italy

0045 ⋯→ Greiner Design Associates
⋯→ USA

0046 ⇢ Hat Trick Design
⇢ UK

0047 ⇢ Hat Trick Design
⇢ UK

0048 ⇢ Hat Trick Design
⇢ UK

0049 ⇢ Frost Design, Sydney
⇢ Australia

0050 ⋯⋗ **Frost Design, Sydney**
      ⋯⋗ Australia

0051 ⇝ **Fitch**
     ⇝ USA

0052 ⇝ **Fitch**
     ⇝ USA

0053 ⇝ **Fitch**
     ⇝ USA

0054 ⇝ **Fitch**
     ⇝ USA

0055 ⋯> Fitch
⋯> USA

0056 ⋯> Walker Group
⋯> USA

0057 ⋯> Fitch
⋯> USA

0058 ⋯> Fitch
⋯> USA

0059 ⟶ Fitch
⟶ USA

0060 ⋯⋟ **Fitch**
⋯⋟ USA

0061 ⋯⟶ Brandhouse WTS
⋯⟶ UK

0062 ⋯⟶ christiansen: creative
⋯⟶ USA

0063 ⋯⟶ A10 Design
⋯⟶ Brazil

0064 ⋯⟶ A10 Design
⋯⟶ Brazil

0065 ⤳ Finest/Magma
  ⤳ Germany

0066 ⋯› Fitch
⋯› USA

0067 ⋯› The Dunlavey Studio
⋯› USA

0068 ⋯› Richard Poulin Design Group
⋯› USA

0069 ⋯› Warm Rain Ltd
⋯› UK

0070 ---> Elfen
---> Wales

0071 ---> Walker Group
---> USA

0072 ---> Pentagram Design
---> USA

0073 ---> Fitch
---> USA

0074 ⇢ R&Mag Graphic Design
⇢ Italy

0075 ⇢ Elfen
⇢ Wales

0076 ⇢ Q
⇢ Germany

0077 ⇢ Q
⇢ Germany

0078 ┈┈▶ Sea Design
　　　┈┈▶ UK

0079 ⋯➔ A10 Design
⋯➔ Brazil

0080 ⋯➔ Hollis Brand Communications
⋯➔ USA

0081 ⋯➔ Brandhouse WTS
⋯➔ UK

0082 ⋯➔ Brandhouse WTS
⋯➔ UK

0083 ⋯⟶ Studio Output
⋯⟶ UK

0084 ⋯⟶ Studio Output
⋯⟶ UK

0085 ⋯⟶ Vital Signs & Graphics
⋯⟶ USA

0086 ⋯⟶ Vital Signs & Graphics
⋯⟶ USA

0087 ⇢ i_d buero
    ⇢ Germany

0088 ⇢ Jonni
    ⇢ Norway

0089 ⇢ Kenneth Diseño
    ⇢ Mexico

0090 ⇢ Jonni
    ⇢ Norway

0091 ⋯→ Pentagram Design
⋯→ USA

0092 ⋯→ Pentagram Design
⋯→ USA

0093 ⋯→ Poulin & Morris
⋯→ USA

0094 ⋯→ Crush Design & Art Direction
⋯→ UK

0096 ⟶ Big Eyes Design
⟶ Israel

0097 ⟶ BigEyes Design
⟶ Israel

0098 ⟶ AdamsMorioka
⟶ USA

0099 ⟶ AdamsMorioka
⟶ USA

01.00 ⋯⇢ bonbon london
⋯⇢ UK

01.01 ⋯⇢ bonbon london
⋯⇢ UK

01.02 ⋯⇢ Taxi Studio Ltd
⋯⇢ UK

01.03 ⋯⇢ Elephant Design Pvt Ltd
⋯⇢ India

01.04 ⋯→ Taxi Studio Ltd
       ⋯→ UK

01.05 ⋯⟩ christiansen: creative
      ⋯⟩ USA

01.06 ⋯⟩ Jonni
      ⋯⟩ Norway

01.07 ⋯⟩ Sea Design
      ⋯⟩ UK

01.08 ⋯⟩ Mimolimit
      ⋯⟩ Czech Republic

01.1.1. ⤑ Minelli, Inc
⤑ USA

01.1.2 ⤑ Minelli, Inc
⤑ USA

01.1.3 ⤑ i_d buero
⤑ Germany

01.1.4 ⤑ Vrontikis Design Office
⤑ USA

0.1.1.5 ⋯➔ Hamagami/Carroll, Inc
⋯➔ USA

0.1.1.6 ⋯➔ Hamagami/Carroll, Inc
⋯➔ USA

0.1.1.7 ⋯➔ Hamagami/Carroll, Inc
⋯➔ USA

0.1.1.8 ⋯➔ Hamagami/Carroll, Inc
• ⋯➔ USA

0119 --> Hamagami/Carroll, Inc
--> USA

01.20 ⋯→ Hollis Brand Communications
⋯→ USA

01.21 ⋯→ Vrontikis Design Office
⋯→ USA

01.22 ⋯→ Vrontikis Design Office
⋯→ USA

01.23 ⋯→ The Dunlavey Studio
⋯→ USA

01.24 --> AdamsMorioka
--> USA

01.25 ⋯› AdamsMorioka
⋯› USA

01.26 ⋯› sky design
⋯› USA

01.27 ⋯› Kenneth Diseño
⋯› Mexico

01.28 ⋯› S&N Design
⋯› USA

01.29 --> Mary Hutchinson Design LLC
--> USA

01.30 --> Mirko Ilić Corp.
--> USA

01.31 --> Mirko Ilić Corp.
--> USA

01.32 --> Mirko Ilić Corp.
--> USA

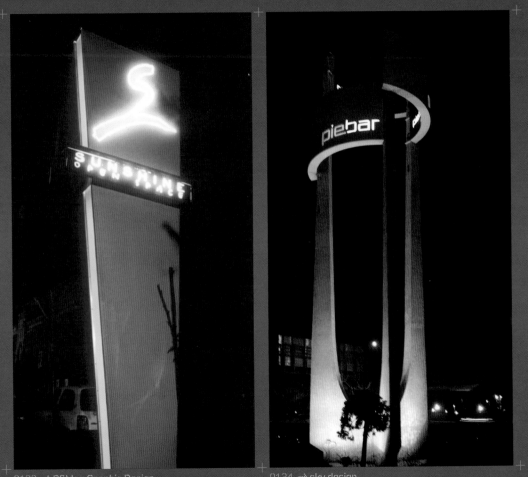

01.33 ⇢ R&Mag Graphic Design
⇢ Italy

01.34 ⇢ sky design
⇢ USA

0135 ⤳ **sky design**
     ⤳ USA

0136 ⋯➔ bonbon london
⋯➔ UK

01.37 ⟶ Damion Hickman Design
⟶ USA

01.38 ⟶ Braue Strategic Brand Design
⟶ Germany

01.39 ⟶ Tharp Did It
⟶ USA

01.40 ⟶ R&Mag Graphic Design
⟶ Italy

0141 ···> Hollis Brand Communications
       ···> USA

0142 ···> R&Mag Graphic Design
       ···> Italy

0143 ···> R&Mag Graphic Design
       ···> Italy

0144 ···> Hornall Anderson Design Works
       ···> USA

0145 --> **Kenneth Diseño**
--> Mexico

0146 --> **Kenneth Diseño**
--> Mexico

0147 --> **Frost Design, Sydney**
--> Australia

0148 --> **Hornall Anderson Design Works**
--> USA

01.49 ⋯⇢ Elfen
       ⋯⇢ Wales

01.50 ⋯⇢ Hollis Brand Communications
       ⋯⇢ USA

01.51 ⋯➤ Tomato Košir
⋯➤ Slovenia

01.52 ⇢ Fullblastinc.com
⇢ USA

01.53 ⇢ The Dunlavey Studio
⇢ USA

01.54 ⇢ The Dunlavey Studio
⇢ USA

01.55 ⇢ The Dunlavey Studio
⇢ USA

01.56 ⋯→ Hollis Brand Communications
⋯→ USA

01.57 ⋯→ John Kneapler Design
⋯→ USA

01.58 ⋯→ Mimolimit
⋯→ Czech Republic

01.59 ⋯→ Hunt Weber Clark Associates
⋯→ USA

01.60 ⟶ Qually & Company
⟶ USA

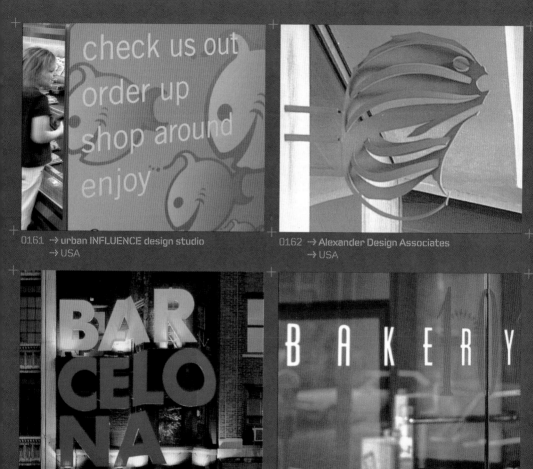

0161 ⋯⋗ urban INFLUENCE design studio
⋯⋗ USA

0162 ⋯⋗ Alexander Design Associates
⋯⋗ USA

0163 ⋯⋗ Marve Cooper Design, Ltd.
⋯⋗ USA

0164 ⋯⋗ Tharp Did It
⋯⋗ USA

01.65 ⋯→ Sayles Graphic Design
⋯→ USA

01.66 ⋯⟶ Les LaMotte Design
⋯⟶ USA

01.67 ⋯⟶ Greteman Group
⋯⟶ USA

01.68 ⋯⟶ Hunt Weber Clark Associates
⋯⟶ USA

01.69 ⋯⟶ The Art Commission, Inc.
⋯⟶ USA

01.70 ⋯➤ Vital Signs & Graphics
⋯➤ USA

0171 ⟶ Evenson Design Group
⟶ USA

0172 ⟶ Pentagram Design
⟶ USA

0173 ⟶ The Invisions Group Ltd.
⟶ USA

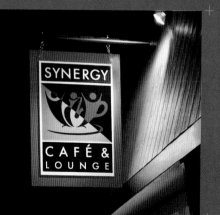

0174 ⟶ Evenson Design Group
⟶ USA

01.75-0398

02

····➤

CHAPTER 2
LOGOS

····➤

0176 ⇢ Studio Output
⇢ UK

0177 ⇢ Studio Output
⇢ UK

0178 ⇢ Mimolimit
⇢ Czech Republic

0179 ⇢ Sea Design
⇢ UK

01.80 ⇢ Etc Diseño Gráfico
⇢ Venezuela

01.81 ⇢ Unreal
⇢ UK

01.82 ⇢ Unreal
⇢ UK

01.83 ⇢ Jonni
⇢ Norway

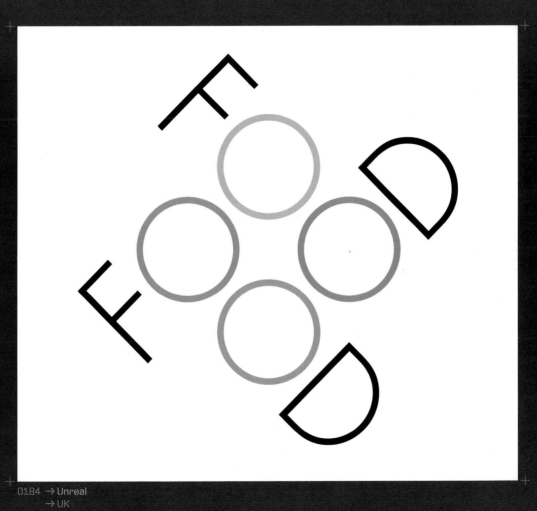

01.85 ⟶ **28 Limited Brand**
   ⟶ Germany

01.86 ⟶ **28 Limited Brand**
   ⟶ Germany

01.87 ⟶ **28 Limited Brand**
   ⟶ Germany

01.88 ⟶ **28 Limited Brand**
   ⟶ Germany

ticklefish

01.90 ⋯➔ urban INFLUENCE design studio
⋯➔ USA

01.91 ⇢ urban INFLUENCE design studio
⇢ USA

01.92 ⇢ BigEyes Design
⇢ Israel

01.93 ⇢ Commarts Inc
⇢ USA

01.94 ⇢ The Jones Group
⇢ USA

01.95 ⇢ Turnstyle
⇢ USA

01.96 ⇢ Tom Varisco Designs
⇢ USA

01.97 ⇢ Kenneth Diseño
⇢ Mexico

01.98 ⇢ Graphicwise Inc
⇢ USA

01.99 ⟶ Kenneth Diseño
⟶ Mexico

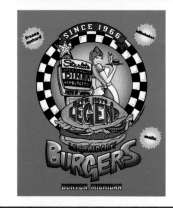

0200 ⇢ The Jones Group
⇢ USA

0201 ⇢ Campus Collection
⇢ USA

0202 ⇢ TD2, Identity & Strategic Design
⇢ Mexico

0203 ⇢ Jeff Fisher LogoMotives
⇢ USA

0206 → Morrow McKenzie Design
→ USA

0207 ⋯› Jeff Fisher LogoMotives
⋯› USA

0208 ⋯› Jeff Fisher LogoMotives
⋯› USA

0209 ⋯› Advance Design Centre
⋯› USA

0210 ⋯› Advance Design Centre
⋯› USA

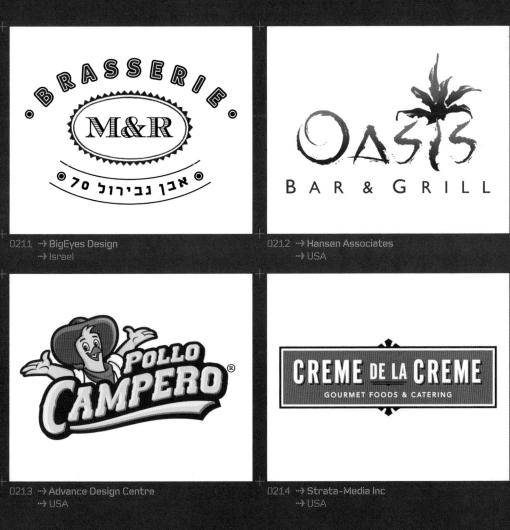

0211 → BigEyes Design
→ Israel

0212 → Hansen Associates
→ USA

0213 → Advance Design Centre
→ USA

0214 → Strata-Media Inc
→ USA

0215 ⟶ Inaria
⟶ UK

0216 ⟶ Sayles Graphic Design
⟶ USA

0217 ⟶ R&Mag Graphic Design
⟶ Italy

0218 ⟶ AdamsMorioka
⟶ USA

0219 ···> Brandhouse WTS
···> UK

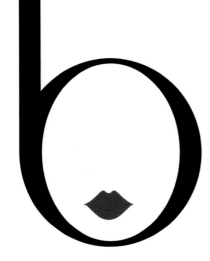

0220 ⟶ From Scratch Design Studio
⟶ USA

0221 ⟶ Dornig Graphic Design
⟶ Austria

THREE BELOW

0223 ⇢ Spark Studio Pty Ltd
⇢ Australia

BERGAMOT CAFE

0225 ⇢ LM
⇢ UK

0226 ⇢ Ph.D
⇢ USA

hacienda

Stiller's

RESTAURANT & BAR

0227 ⇢ Re-Public
⇢ Denmark

0228 ⇢ Q
⇢ Germany

0229 ⇢ The Jones Group
⇢ USA

0230 ⇢ The Jones Group
⇢ USA

0231 ⇢ Vrontikis Design Office
⇢ USA

0232 ⇢ Raidy Printing Group SAL
⇢ Lebanon

0233 ⟶ Taxi Studio Ltd
⟶ UK

0234 ⟶ Q
⟶ Germany

0235 ⟶ LM

0236 ⟶ CDI Studios

0238 ⇢ Bowhaus Design Groupe
⇢ USA

0239 ⋯⟶ Ultra Design
   ⋯⟶ Brazil

0240 ⋯⟶ Advance Design Centre
   ⋯⟶ USA

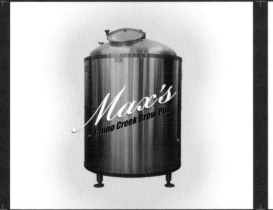

0241 ⋯⟶ Fullblastinc.com
   ⋯⟶ USA

0242 ⋯⟶ Gingerbee Creative
   ⋯⟶ USA

VINO VOYAGE

WINES TO MATCH YOUR MOOD

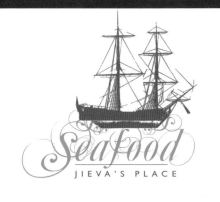

0244 → Laguna College of Art & Design
→ USA

0245 → Prejean Creative
→ USA

0246 → Prejean Creative
→ USA

0247 → Crush Design & Art Direction
→ UK

0248 ⋯→ Prejean Creative
⋯→ USA

0249 ⋯→ Art Institute of California, Orange County
⋯→ USA

0250 ⋯→ VINE360
⋯→ USA

0251 ⋯→ BigEyes Design
⋯→ Israel

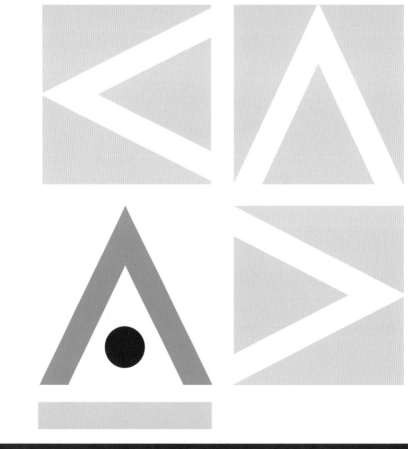

jillbartlett

CAFETER₁A
Ladbroke Grove London W10

0254 ⇢ bonbon london
⇢ UK

0255 ⇢ bonbon london
⇢ UK

G O T H A M

0256 ⇢ Gabriel Kalach - Visual Communication
⇢ USA

0257 ⇢ Studio Siereeni
⇢ USA

0258 ⇢ Smart Works
⇢ Australia

0259 ⇢ Finest/Magma
⇢ Germany

0260 ⇢ Lodge Design
⇢ USA

0261 ⇢ Finest/Magma
⇢ Germany

BAR > LOUNGE

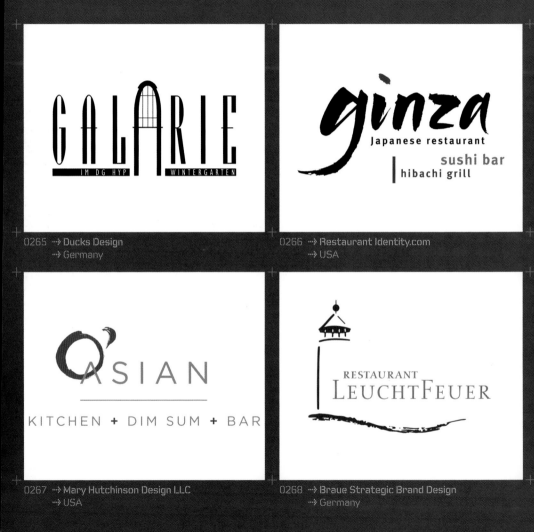

0265 ⇢ Ducks Design
⇢ Germany

0266 ⇢ Restaurant Identity.com
⇢ USA

0267 ⇢ Mary Hutchinson Design LLC
⇢ USA

0268 ⇢ Braue Strategic Brand Design
⇢ Germany

RASIKA
FLAVORS OF INDIA

THE wine bar

0269 ⤳ From Scratch Design Studio
⤳ USA

0270 ⤳ R&Mag Graphic Design
⤳ Italy

titanic
luncheonette · caterer
445 st.pierre, montreal · tel. 849-0894

LOUNGE · BAR

0271 ⤳ Ducks Design

0272 ⤳ Heinzle Design

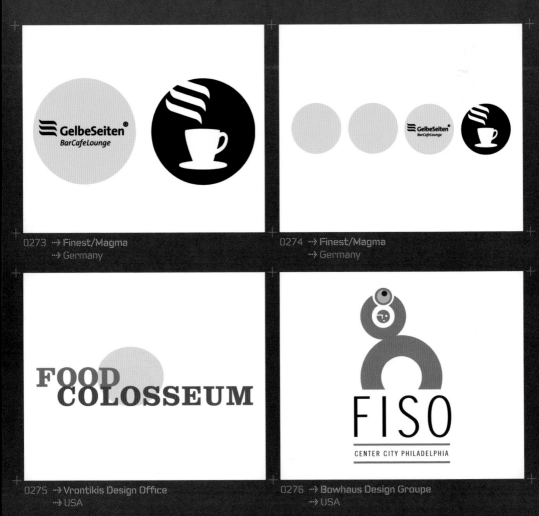

0273 ⋯⟩ Finest/Magma
⋯⟩ Germany

0274 ⋯⟩ Finest/Magma
⋯⟩ Germany

0275 ⋯⟩ Vrontikis Design Office
⋯⟩ USA

0276 ⋯⟩ Bowhaus Design Groupe
⋯⟩ USA

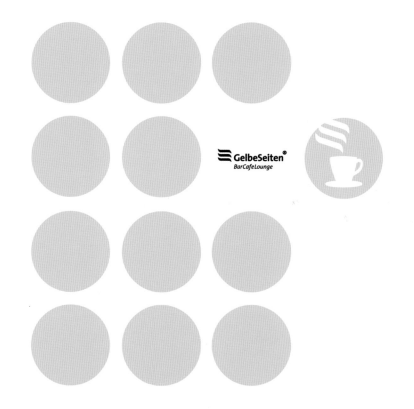

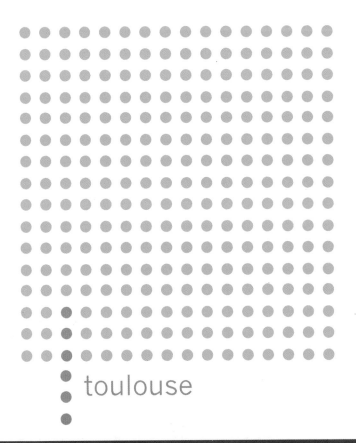

0279 ⟶ Lorenza Zanni
⟶ Italy

0280 ⟶ Warm Rain Ltd
⟶ UK

0281 ⟶ CDI Studios
⟶ USA

0282 ⟶ Mark Frankel Design, Inc
⟶ USA

l'auberge

THE **PERKY PARROT**

0285 ⋯⟶ Sayles Graphic Design
⋯⟶ USA

0286 ⋯⟶ Sayles Graphic Design
⋯⟶ USA

0287 ⋯⟶ The Jones Group
⋯⟶ USA

0288 ⋯⟶ Eye Speak
⋯⟶ USA

0289 ⟶ Octavo Design Pty Ltd
     ⟶ Australia

0290 ⟶ Oliver Russell
     ⟶ USA

0291 ⟶ AdamsMorioka
     ⟶ USA

0292 ⟶ Prejean Creative
     ⟶ USA

0294 ---> Commarts Inc
       ---> USA

0295 ---> Sayles Graphic Design
       ---> USA

0296 ---> S&N Design
       ---> USA

0297 ---> Bullet Communications Inc.
       ---> USA

Vue de Monde

pieros
RESTAURANT & CLUB

1000 Restaurant, Bar and Cafe Graphics
Kimberly Boyd Vickrey
Pieros.eps
704 kb
8.5 x 11
320 dpi

indulge

VERVE

0303 ⋯→ Dean Johnson Design
      ⋯→ USA

0305 ⟶ TD2, Identity & Strategic Design
⟶ Mexico

0306 ⟶ Fresh Oil
⟶ USA

0307 ⟶ Fresh Oil
⟶ USA

0308 ⟶ Fresh Oil
⟶ USA

0309 ⤳ Lodge Design Company
⤳ USA

0310 ⤳ Kenneth Diseño
⤳ Mexico

0311 ⤳ Gabriel Kalach - Visual Communication
⤳ USA

0312 ⤳ Fresh Oil
⤳ USA

0313 ···› Thielen Designs
···› USA

0314 ···› Stanley Moscowitz
···› USA

0315 ···› Fresh Oil
···› USA

0316 ···› CDI Studios
···› USA

0317 ⇢ Dean Johnson Design
⇢ USA

0318 ⇢ Gabriel Kalach - Visual Communication
⇢ USA

0319 ⇢ Mark Frankel Design, Inc
⇢ USA

0320 ⇢ Regan Blough
⇢ USA

0321 ⇢ Thielen Designs
⇢ USA

0322 ⇢ Thielen Designs
⇢ USA

Kanela

BAKERY · CAFÉ · FINE FOODS

0323 ⋯⟩ Octavo Design Pty Ltd
⋯⟩ Australia

0324 ⋯⟩ CDI Studios
⋯⟩ USA

Madison's

RESTAURANT AND WINE GARDEN

OSTERIA DI TRAMONTO™

0325 ⋯⟩ The Jones Group
⋯⟩ USA

0326 ⋯⟩ The Jones Group
⋯⟩ USA

THE BEAN COUNTER

VEGGIE DELI & SOUP BAR

0329 ⋯⟶ CDI Studios
⋯⟶ USA

0330 ⋯⟶ Oliver Russell
⋯⟶ USA

0331 ⋯⟶ Vrontikis Design Office
⋯⟶ USA

0332 ⋯⟶ Ducks Design
⋯⟶ Germany

0333 ⋯▸ Damion Hickman Design
     ⋯▸ USA

SAPORI D'ITALIA
ristorante

ASIAN BISTRO

0335 ⋯⇢ Damion Hickman Design
⋯⇢ USA

0336 ⋯⇢ Damion Hickman Design
⋯⇢ USA

0337 ⋯⇢ Campus Collection
⋯⇢ USA

0338 ⋯⇢ Campus Collection
⋯⇢ USA

SUTRA

0339 → TD2, Identity & Strategic Design
→ Mexico

YuSHan

0340 → TD2, Identity & Strategic Design
→ Mexico

CHIN-AI

0341 → TD2, Identity & Strategic Design
→ Mexico

fusion
at pdc

0342 → AdamsMorioka
→ USA

0343 ⋯→ Rome & Gold Creative
⋯→ USA

0344 ⋯→ David Caunce
⋯→ UK

0345 ⋯→ Fresh Oil
⋯→ USA

0346 ⋯→ Fresh Oil
⋯→ USA

Décadence du
Chocolat

0347 ⟶ Vrontikis Design Office
⟶ USA

0349 ⇢ Commarts Inc
⇢ USA

0350 ⇢ Vrontikis Design Office
⇢ USA

0351 ⇢ Kenneth Diseño
⇢ Mexico

0352 ⇢ i_d buero
⇢ Germany

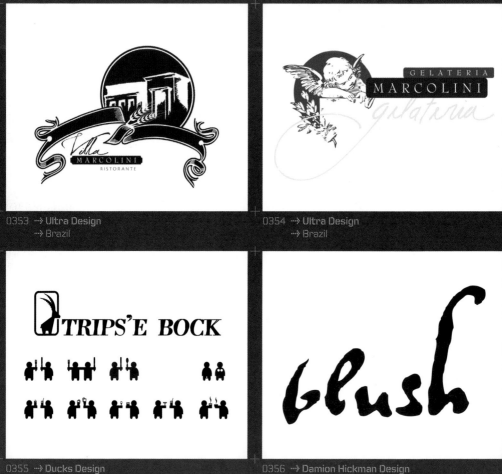

0353 ⇢ Ultra Design
   ⇢ Brazil

0354 ⇢ Ultra Design
   ⇢ Brazil

0355 ⇢ Ducks Design
   ⇢ Germany

0356 ⇢ Damion Hickman Design
   ⇢ USA

0359 Fresh Oil
USA

0360 Rome & Gold Creative
USA

0361 Restaurant Identity.com
USA

0362 Restaurant Identity.com
USA

0363 ⋯⇢ Kenneth Diseño
⋯⇢ Mexico

0364 ⋯⇢ Kenneth Diseño
⋯⇢ Mexico

0365 ⋯⇢ Kenneth Diseño
⋯⇢ Mexico

0366 ⋯⇢ Kenneth Diseño
⋯⇢ Mexico

0367 ⇢ **Kenneth Diseño**
    ⇢ Mexico

0368 ⇢ **Kenneth Diseño**
    ⇢ Mexico

0369 ⇢ **Kenneth Diseño**
    ⇢ Mexico

0370 ⇢ **Kenneth Diseño**
    ⇢ Mexico

0373 ⋯⟶ Fresh Oil
⋯⟶ USA

0374 ⋯⟶ Vrontikis Design Office
⋯⟶ USA

0375 ⋯⟶ Fresh Oil
⋯⟶ USA

0376 ⋯⟶ Fresh Oil
⋯⟶ USA

0377 ⋯→ R&Mag Graphic Design
⋯→ Italy

0378 ⋯→ Minelli, Inc
⋯→ USA

0379 ⋯→ Ducks Design
⋯→ Germany

0380 ⋯→ Jeff Fisher LogoMotives
⋯→ USA

THE
COCK AND
2005
TRUMPET

TOTTem

0386 ⋯➤ Regan Blough
⋯➤ USA

0387 ⋯➤ Mixer
⋯➤ Switzerland

0388 ⋯➤ The Jones Group
⋯➤ USA

0389 ⋯➤ Restaurant Identity.com
⋯➤ USA

0390 ⟶ Campus Collection
⟶ USA

0391 ⟶ Braue Strategic Brand Design
⟶ Germany

tea house

0392 ⟶ The Invisions Group Ltd.
⟶ USA

0393 ⟶ LM
⟶ UK

0394 ⟶ Gabriel Kalach - Visual Communication
⟶ USA

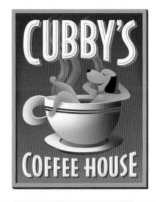

0395 ⋯→ Rickabaugh Graphics
⋯→ USA

0396 ⋯→ Evenson Design Group
⋯→ USA

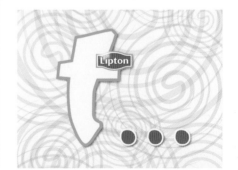

0397 ⋯→ Evenson Design Group
⋯→ USA

0398 ⋯→ Elephant Design Pvt Ltd
⋯→ India

CHAPTER 3
MENUS

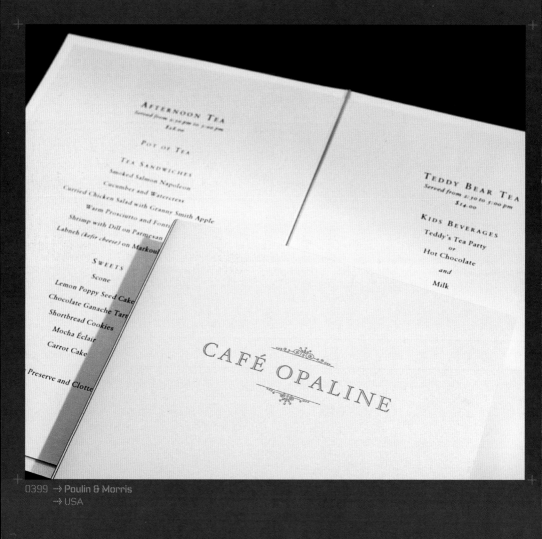

0400 ⋯⟶ Minelli, Inc
⋯⟶ USA

0401 ⋯⟶ Taxi Studio Ltd
⋯⟶ UK

0402 ⋯⟶ i_d buero
⋯⟶ Germany

0403 ⋯⟶ i_d buero
⋯⟶ Germany

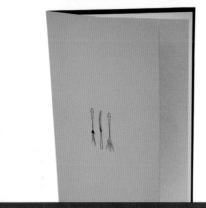

0404 → The Design Laboratory
→ UK

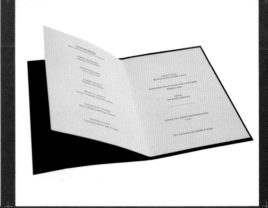

0405 → The Design Laboratory
→ UK

0406 → The Design Laboratory
→ UK

0407 → The Design Laboratory
→ UK

0409 ···▸ urban INFLUENCE design studio
···▸ USA

0410 ···▸ urban INFLUENCE design studio
···▸ USA

0411 ⇢ Studio Output
⇢ UK

0412 ⇢ Ayse Çelem
⇢ Turkey

0413 ⇢ Ayse Çelem
⇢ Turkey

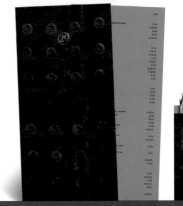

0414 ⇢ Ayse Çelem
⇢ Turkey

0416 ---> Mirko Ilić Corp.
---> USA

0417 ---> Fabrice Praeger
---> France

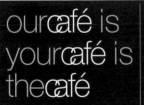

0418 ---> bonbon london
---> UK

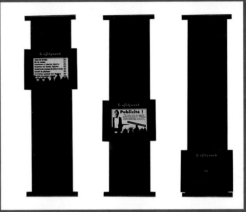

0419 ---> bonbon london
---> UK

0420 → 804© Graphic Design
      → Germany

0421 → Jonni
      → Norway

0422 → biz-R
      → UK

0423 → biz-R
      → UK

0426 ⇢ Crush Design & Art Direction
⇢ UK

0427 ⇢ Crush Design & Art Direction
⇢ UK

0428 ⇢ Morrow McKenzie Design
⇢ USA

0429 ⇢ Lodge Design Company
⇢ USA

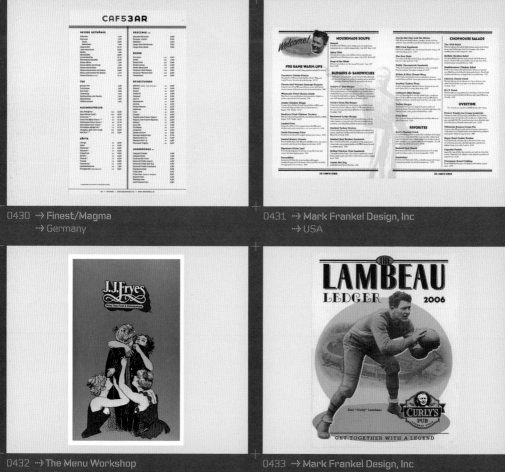

0430 ⇢ Finest/Magma
⇢ Germany

0431 ⇢ Mark Frankel Design, Inc
⇢ USA

0432 ⇢ The Menu Workshop
⇢ USA

0433 ⇢ Mark Frankel Design, Inc
⇢ USA

0434 ⇢ LM
⇢ UK

0435 ⇢ Rickabaugh Graphics
⇢ USA

0436 ⇢ Mimolimit
⇢ Czech Republic

0437 ⇢ Mimolimit
⇢ Czech Republic

0438 ⤍ Mark Frankel Design, Inc
⤍ USA

0439 ⇢ Studio Output
⇢ UK

0440 ⇢ Studio Output
⇢ UK

0441 ⇢ Threefold
⇢ Australia

0442 ⇢ Spark Studio Pty Ltd
⇢ Australia

0443 ⟶ Loewy
⟶ UK

0444 ⟶ Loewy
⟶ UK

0445 ⟶ Loewy
⟶ UK

0446 ⟶ Loewy
⟶ UK

0447 ---> Bakken Creative Company
---> USA

0449 ···> bonbon london
···> UK

0450 ···> bonbon london
···> UK

0451 ···> bonbon london
···> UK

0452 ···> Mirko Ilić Corp.
···> USA

0453 ⋯⋗ David Caunce
⋯⋗ UK

0454 ⋯⋗ David Caunce
⋯⋗ UK

0455 ⋯⋗ David Caunce
⋯⋗ UK

0456 ⋯⋗ David Caunce
⋯⋗ UK

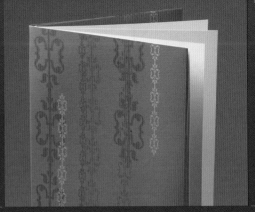

0458 ⇢ Public
　　⇢ USA

0459 ⇢ Public
　　⇢ USA

0460 ⇢ Public
　　⇢ USA

0461 ⇢ Public
　　⇢ USA

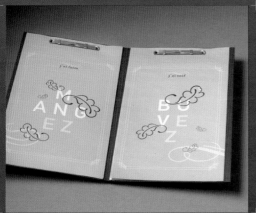

0464 ···> Public
···> USA

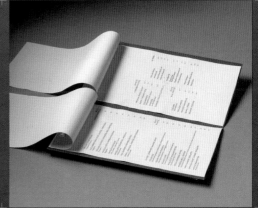

0465 ···> Public
···> USA

0466 ···> Public
···> USA

0467 ···> Public
···> USA

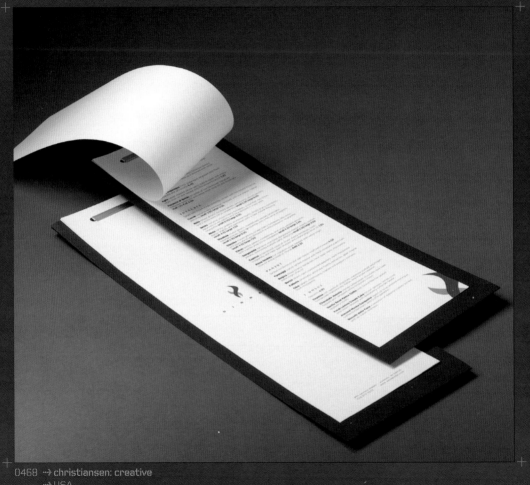

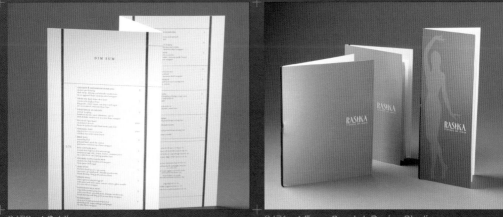

0470 ···> Public
    ···> USA

0471 ···> From Scratch Design Studio
    ···> USA

0472 ···> Bakken Creative Company
    ···> USA

0473 ···> BASELINE
    ···> Scotland

0474 ···> 804© Graphic Design
···> Germany

0475 ···> 804© Graphic Design
···> Germany

0476 ···> 804© Graphic Design
···> Germany

0477 ···> 804© Graphic Design
···> Germany

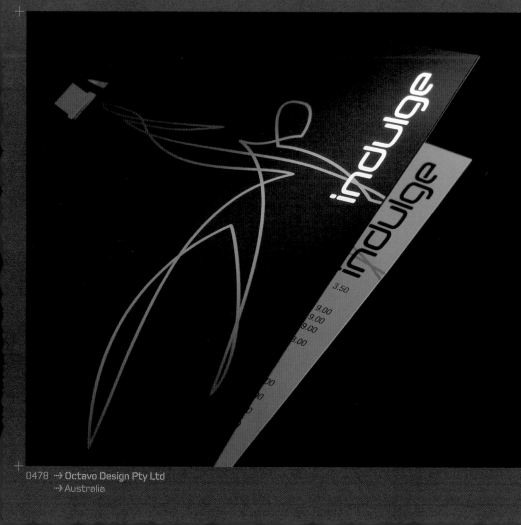

0478 ⇢ Octavo Design Pty Ltd
⇢ Australia

0479 ···⟩ **AdamsMorioka**
      ···⟩ USA

0480 ···⟩ **Graphic Content**
      ···⟩ USA

0481 ···⟩ **Graphic Content**
      ···⟩ USA

0482 ···⟩ **Octavo Design Pty Ltd**
      ···⟩ Australia

3 breakfasts at the 120 days

143 choices at the 120 days

0483 ⇢ Mimolimit
⇢ Czech Republic

0484 ⇢ Mimolimit
⇢ Czech Republic

Tapas

01 5 druhů tapasů podávaných s domácí Focaccia
5 kinds of tapas served with home made Focaccia
160 Kč — 6.40 €

02 Košík chleba nebo Foccacia
Bread basket or Foccacia
35 Kč — 1.40 €

Polévka
Soup

03 Smetanová houbová polévka
Creamy mushroom soup
110 Kč — 4.40 €

04 Gaspaccio studená polévka
Gaspaccio cold soup
90 Kč — 3.60 €

Předkrmy
Starters

05 Hovězí Carpaccio s rukolou a hruškami
Beef carpaccio with pears, rocket leaves
and balsamic
180 Kč — 7.20 €

06 Sušené hovězí carpaccio
Dried beef carpaccio
310 Kč — 12.40 €

07 Sýrový talíř
French cheese plate
150 Kč — 6.00 €

08 Meloun s feta sýrem
Watermelon with feta cheese
110 Kč — 4.40 €

09 Italský talíř
Italian plate
230 Kč — 9.20 €

10 Křupavé kalamáry s mořskou solí a chilli
Crispy calamari with rock salt and chilli
165 Kč — 6.60 €

Hlavní jídla
Main courses

11 Club burger se slaninou, sýrem čedar, rajčaty
a hlávkovým salátem
Club burger with bacon, cheddar,
tomatoes and lettuce
240 Kč — 9.60 €

12 Francouzský burger s restovanou foie gras
a grilovanými houbami
French burger served with seared foie gras
and grilled mushrooms
290 Kč — 11.60 €

13 Kuřecí křídýlka s karamelovou chilli omáčkou
Chicken wings with chilli-caramel sauce
130 Kč — 5.20 €

14 Nabídka z křupavých Dim-Sum
se sladkou chilli omáčkou
Assortment of crispy Dim-Sum
with sweet chilli sauce
155 Kč — 6.20 €

Dezerty
Desserts

15 Tvarohový dort „New York style"
N.Y. style cheesecake
110 Kč — 4.40 €

16 Kokosové tiramisu
Coconut tiramisu
125 Kč — 5 €

17 Horký čokoládový dort
Hot chocolate cake
125 Kč — 5 €

18 Banana loty
Thai banana pancake
110 Kč — 4.40 €

19 Ovocný talíř
Fruits plate
120 Kč — 4.80 €

20 Variace zmrzliny
Variation of ice cream
80 Kč — 3.20 €

Děkujeme Vám za návštěvu restaurace 120 days.
Thank you for visiting restaurant 120 days.

47 nights at the 120 days

70 wines at the 120 days
47 nights at the 120 days

0487 ⟶ McCord Graphic Design
⟶ Country unavailable

0488 ⟶ Val Gene Associates
⟶ USA

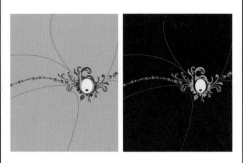

0489 ⟶ From Scratch Design Studio
⟶ USA

0490 ⟶ Brandhouse WTS
⟶ UK

coffeeBAR

0493 ···> BigEyes Design
···> USA

0494 ···> BigEyes Design
···> USA

0495 ···> BigEyes Design
···> USA

0496 ···> BigEyes Design
···> USA

PORT & SHERRY
By the Glass

Sandeman	27	סנדמן
Sandeman Sherry Don Fino	30	סנדמן שרי דון פינו
Fonesca Bin 27	34	פונסקה בין 27
Fonesca Vintage 86	60	פונסקה וינטאג' 86
Otima	29	אוטימה
Tio Pepe Sherry	28	טיו פפה שרי
Drysack Oloroso 15	33	אלורוסו 15
Don Guido Pedro Ximenez 20	33	פדרו חימנז 20
Jalifa Amontillado 30	38	אמונטיאדו 30
Pineau des Charentes	25	פינו דה שאראנט

0497 ⟶ BigEyes Design
⟶ USA

Dessert Menu

קרם ברולה 32

טירמיסו 34
שכבות עוגיי באספרסו וקום, ובינה וגבינת מסקרפונה

קנולי 28
בסילי גביתת רוקוטה מתוקה וקולפות תמוזים מסוקרות

פירות קריס 36
פירות העטה עם תטת תות, גלידת פיל ורובנים בבורזי

מיל אפייום 28
גלידת וניל ושוקולד בבורזי

שטרודל בוונה 36
עם שקדים ואגוזי לוז ברוסק שופי גלידת פיל

טטת שוקולד 32

טופה שוקולד 34

PORT & SHERRY
By the Glass

Sandeman	27	סנדמן
Sandeman Sherry Don Fino	30	סנדמן שרי דון פינו
Fonesca Bin 27	34	פונסקה בין 27
Fonesca Vintage 86	60	פונסקה וינטאג' 86
Otima	29	אוטימה
Tio Pepe Sherry	28	טיו פפה שרי
Drysack Oloroso 15	33	אלורוסו 15
Don Pedro Ximenez 20	33	פדרו חימנז 20
Jalifa Amontillado 30	38	אמונטיאדו 30
Pineau des Charentes	25	פינו דה שאראנט

DESSERT WINES

Tokaji Oremus Aszu 4 Puttyonus 98
טוקאי, אורמוס אסו 98
25/160 ....

בוצא רוה 36
אם קרם שטנילי ז'אנוס טו רקמל

מייל לוי שוקולד 38
עז קנט שונה

מבריבה

עם קרם מסקרי תוחום מסוקרוס 38
צלחת קראמלסיס

עם שקרים עם אנשם, מרום לימון 38
ובסקרי עם פירות שר

0498 ⟶ BigEyes Design
⟶ USA

NewYear Night 31.12.05

רגולי של תרד גבינת שירם עם עגבניות קטמרי וקרמל ראשמו 45

שלם עלים אביבית עם גרעת פריליון ועטר בוטקה בירוטה המחית ושאט אנדי לוז 52

לבנת חטמ ערבית ברוטם קטר עם ביקן וקרנל 48

עיקריות

פילה אמטר יע על ארסרטקים העירא מ פיל לוז והפתאת 110

פילה לקטת עם בוק-ב'ר על מאדירל, בצר דרמ-היה 120

קרופ פירות ש - קלתורי, חתילת שוצפרה מ'אבו שר'אסק

שרירים המתבו, בצר ממודית והעמר 130

דיקר שרישטת עם ממקרטרת ורישו, בציר שרוב'א והגברנ קלחית 116

את קומר עם האוזה מתמתנת על אמבוטי ארבה ברהבלים ואמבונאל בבחתה חמת 86

פילה בצר עם פות עם בצ, עם ממונת ותקבור עם בצר המרותב'ו, יור אמונד 120

אטרדוקם של פתת פר יעם מתות ותקבולו של פרת ב מרור 135

עלחת ע'ראני על יחלד גולרי, עמבית קלדרא חמתה אבוטה בעט ....

0499 ⟶ BigEyes Design
⟶ USA

Chamapagne & Sparklin

White

Red

Dessert

Wine Special

Ariola Brut (375 ml)	130
שרים ברוט שמפניה 375 מל	
Bollinger Special Cuvee Brut	400
בולינגר שפ'של קום ברום	
Masi Serego Alighieri, Possessant Bianco 04	119/53
מאסי סרגו אליגירי, פוסשסנ'ז ביאנקו 04	
Yarden Katzrin, Chardonnay 03	129/36
ירדן קצרין, שרדונה 03	
Chablis Grand Cru Vaudesir 89	299
שאבלי גרא קרו וודזיר 89	
Yarden Cabernet Sauvignon 03	149/39
ירדן קברנה סוביניון 03	
Allegrini Palazzo Della Torre 00	175/45
אלגרני פלצ'ו דלה טורה 00	
Tommasi Amarone Della Valpolicella 00	249
טומסי אמרונה דלה ואלפוליצ'לה 00	
Chateau Bouyot Sauternes 81	25
שאטו בויו סוטרן 81	

NewYear Night 31.12.05

0500 ⟶ BigEyes Design
⟶ USA

0502 ⇢ Allies
⇢ UK

0503 ⇢ Allies
⇢ UK

0504 ⇢ Allies
⇢ UK

0505 ⇢ Allies
⇢ UK

0508 ---> Rome & Gold Creative
---> USA

0509 ---> Brandhouse WTS
---> UK

0510 ---> Brandhouse WTS
---> UK

0511 ---> Brandhouse WTS
---> UK

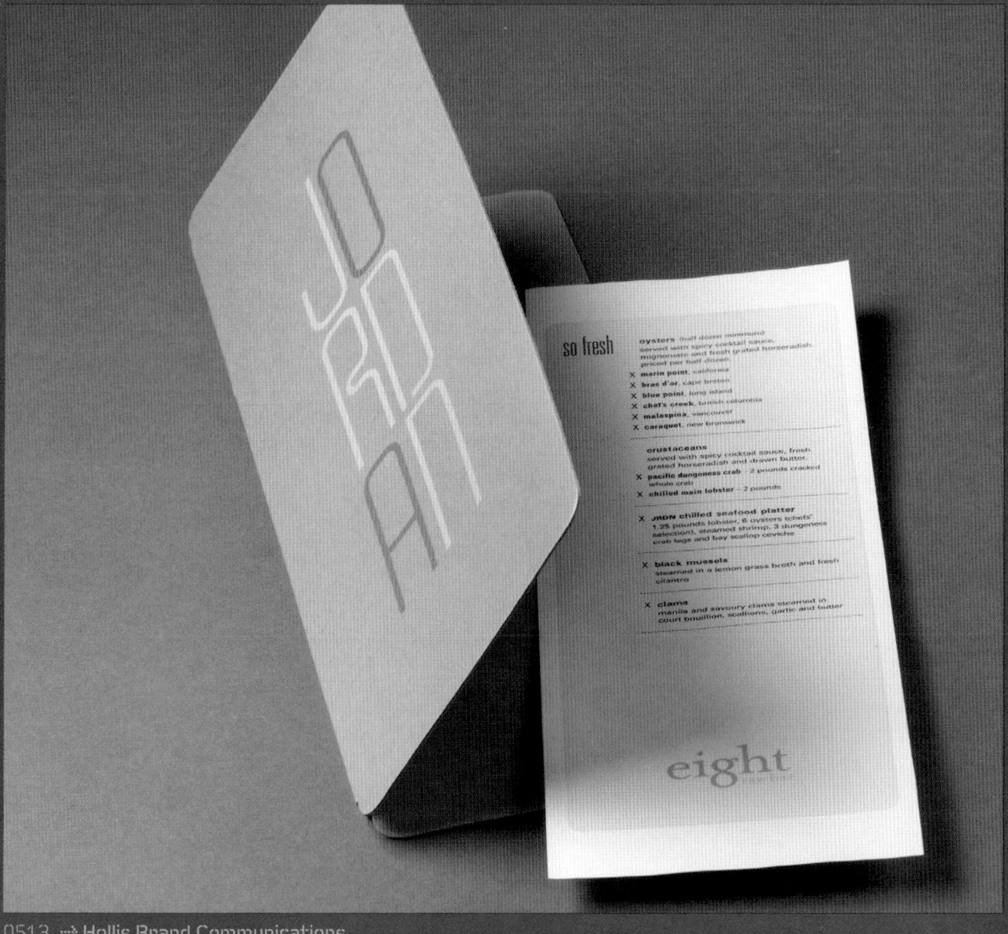

0513 Hollis Brand Communications
USA

0514 ···> **Braue Strategic Brand Design**
···> Germany

0515 ···> **Braue Strategic Brand Design**
···> Germany

0516 ···> **A1.0 Design**
···> Brazil

0517 ···> **A1.0 Design**
···> Brazil

0518 ---> **R&Mag Graphic Design**
    ---> Italy

0519 ---> **Associates Design**
    ---> USA

0520 ---> **bonbon london**
    ---> UK

0521 ---> **Hardy Design**
    ---> Brazil

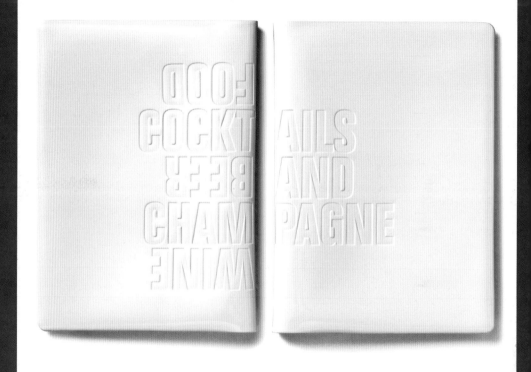

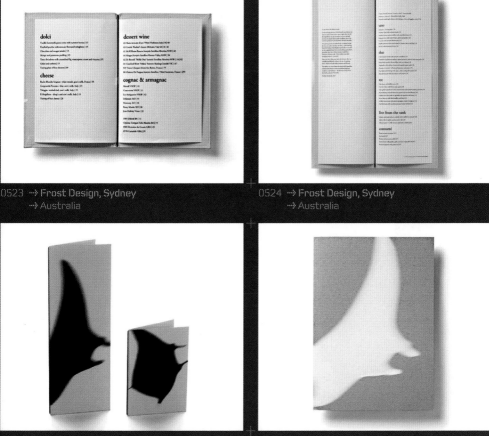

0523 ---> **Frost Design, Sydney**
---> Australia

0524 ---> **Frost Design, Sydney**
---> Australia

0525 ---> **Frost Design, Sydney**
---> Australia

0526 ---> **Frost Design, Sydney**
---> Australia

0527 ⇢ Fullblastinc.com
⇢ USA

0528 ⇢ Fullblastinc.com
⇢ USA

0529 ⇢ Brandhouse WTS
⇢ UK

0530 ⇢ Public
⇢ USA

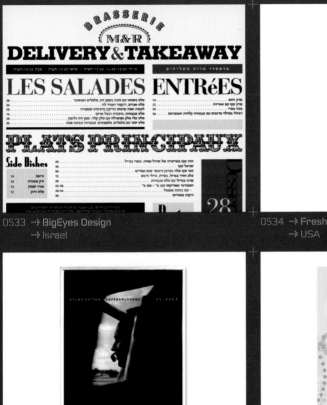

0533 ⇢ BigEyes Design
    ⇢ Israel

0534 ⇢ Fresh Oil
    ⇢ USA

0535 ⇢ Finest/Magma
    ⇢ Germany

0536 ⇢ Fresh Oil
    ⇢ USA

0537 → BigEyes Design
→ Israel

0538 → BigEyes Design
→ Israel

0539 → BigEyes Design
→ Israel

0540 → BigEyes Design
→ Israel

0542 ⋯➔ Ducks Design
⋯➔ Germany

0543 ⋯➔ Ducks Design
⋯➔ Germany

0544 ⋯➔ Restaurant Identity.com
⋯➔ USA

0545 ⋯➔ Ducks Design
⋯➔ Germany

Our Taste Specialists have been working hard to map the variety of flavors available at Sheridan's. Now you can mix up your favorite flavors for your own unique Treat DNA.

0548 ⤏ Hollis Brand Communications
⤏ USA

0549 ⤏ Willoughby Design Group
⤏ USA

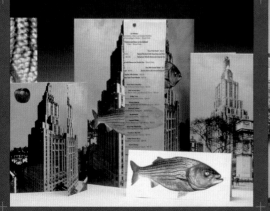

0550 ⤏ Pentagram Design
⤏ USA

0551 ⤏ Hornall Anderson Design Works
⤏ USA

0552 ⋯→ On The Edge Design, Inc
⋯→ USA

0553 ⇢ On The Edge Design, Inc
⇢ USA

0554 → Fullblastinc.com
→ USA

0555 → S&N Design
→ USA

0556 → Disney Design Group
→ USA

0557 → christiansen: creative
→ USA

0558 ⇢ Associates Design
⇢ USA

0559 ⇢ Associates Design
⇢ USA

0560 ⇢ Lance Anderson Design
⇢ USA

0561 ⇢ John & Orna Designs
⇢ UK

0562 ⋯→ Heinzle Design
⋯→ Austria

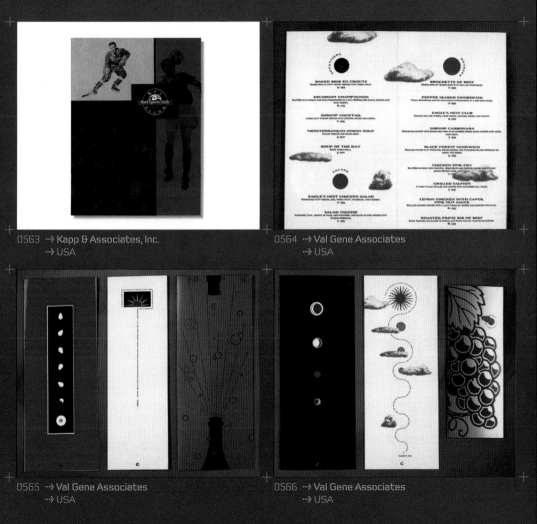

0563 ⋯➤ Kapp & Associates, Inc.
⋯➤ USA

0564 ⋯➤ Val Gene Associates
⋯➤ USA

0565 ⋯➤ Val Gene Associates
⋯➤ USA

0566 ⋯➤ Val Gene Associates
⋯➤ USA

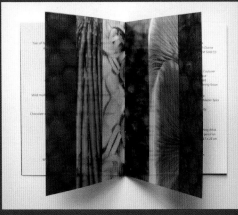

0567 ⋯→ John & Orna Designs
⋯→ UK

0568 ⋯→ John & Orna Designs
⋯→ UK

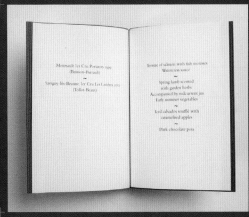

0569 ⋯→ John & Orna Designs
⋯→ UK

0570 ⋯→ John & Orna Designs
⋯→ UK

HAZEL AND DAVID ~ THE DECADES
Saturday 14 May 2005

0571 --> John & Orna Designs
--> UK

La tartine

LES TARTINES SALÉES
(servi avec marinade style grand-maman)

LaQuerbes
Rôti de bœuf froid, gruyère, compote d'oignons au balsamique, figue noire et sauce maison

LaBloomfield
Gravlax de saumon King bio, lard fumé, épinards et émulsion au galanga

LaChampagneur
Jambon de Parme, aubergines chinoises marinées, ricotta et sauce miso

LaWiseman
Thon Saku cru, avocat haché au couteau, yuzu, verdure et mayonnaise au piment d'Espelette

LaStuart
Volaille de grain grillée, yogourt aux tomates confites à la sarriette et au fromage Manchego

LES TARTINES SUCRÉES

LaPommeCaramel
Compote de pommes Empire et cannelle en bâton, beurre fermier, caramel au Jack Daniel's

LaFraiseSzechuan
Purée de fraises au poivre de szechuan, fromage blanc à la lime et sucre en pain râpé

LaMarmelade
Marmelade d'agrumes mi-sucrée, crème fleurette à la truffe blanche

LA DENT SUCRÉE

LeFinancier
Financier tiède aux amandes de clémentines entières en purée et crème cuite à la cassonade

LaCrème
Crème brûlée classique à la vanille

LePannaCotta
Panna cotta au café, yogourt biologique nature et sablé à la cardamome

LeBiscuit
Biscuit davoine, ganache au chocolat noir de cacao (75%) et confiture de lait

SOUPES

LePanais
Crème de panais, huile de cari de Madras, brunoise de pomme fruit Golden et sel de céleri

LaLentille
Soupe de lentilles verte du Puy, pommes de terre ratte, légumes verts du moment et crème sûre au paprika fumé

LaPoule
Bouillon de poule bien réduit, orge biologique, pancetta rôtie et beaucoup de persil simple

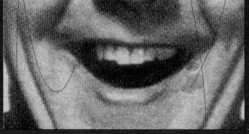

La tartine

SALADES

Lépinard
Épinard bébé, antipasti, pamplemousse Ruby, menthe en feuille, vinaigrette minute au yogourt nature et miel de pommier

LaBette
Betteraves cuites entières, cresson, noix de pin rôties, huile de pistache première pression et vin cotto italien

LaRémoul
Rémoulade de légumes d'hiver, émulsion classique au citron, caperon et œuf de caille mariné au vieux xérès

LaFenouil
Copeaux de fenouil, tomates confites au sucre brut, macédoine de poire japonaise, huile de piment oiseau et pralin au sésame

LaBourbon
Mélange de laitue selon la saison, vinaigrette au cidre de glace et marinade d'oignons à la vanille Bourbon

PLATEAUX DE FROMAGE SELON L'ARRIVAGE ET GARNITURE STYLE TARTINE

(Purée de raisins rouges, noisettes rôties et croûtons de pain au noix)

LES GRILLES-FROMAGE

(choix de pains: grains germés bio, intégral bio, kamut bio ou classique bio)

LeVanHorne
Ketchup maison aux tomates épicées (vanille, cannelle, cumin, poivre), Victor et Berthold, amandes rôties d'Espagne et jeune pousse

LeLajoie
Purée de dattes de Mejold, compoté au poivre long, bacon fumé, vieux cheddar de l'Isle-aux-Grues

LeBernard
Chorizo XXX grillé, oignon sucré caramélisé, moutarde à la bière, chèvre noir vieilli

LeSt-Viateur
Légumes grillés au thym frais et marinés à l'huile d'olive au citron, fromage en grains

LeFairmount
Tomates séchées marinées, confit de canard au laurier, chèvre frais non-affiné et huile d'ail confit

LeLaurier
Salami à cru, fromage Pied-de-vent, purée d'herbe à la fleur de sel, abricot hydraté

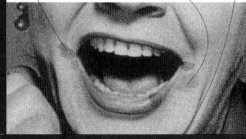

0574 ---> Heather Heflin
---> USA

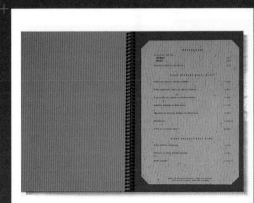

0575 ---> Heather Heflin
---> USA

0576 ---> David Carter Design
---> USA

0577 ---> David Carter Design
---> USA

0578 ⇢ Mary Hutchinson Design LLC
⇢ USA

0579 ···> Val Gene Associates
···> USA

0580 ···> Val Gene Associates
···> USA

0581 ···> Val Gene Associates
···> USA

0582 ···> Sagmeister Inc.
···> USA

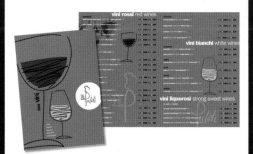

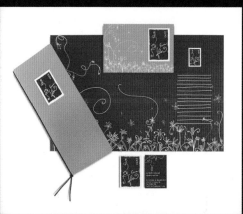

0583 ⇢ bonbon london
    ⇢ UK

0584 ⇢ R&Mag Graphic Design
    ⇢ Italy

0585 ⇢ Hardy Design
    ⇢ Brazil

0586 ⇢ R&Mag Graphic Design
    ⇢ Italy

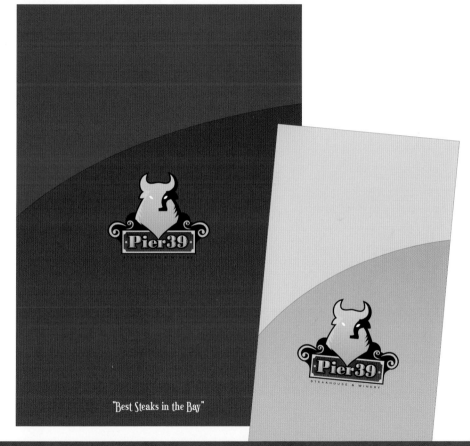

"Best Steaks in the Bay"

0587 ⋯⟶ Graphicwise Inc
⋯⟶ USA

0588 ⋯→ Hollis Brand Communications
     ⋯→ USA

0589 ···› Hollis Brand Communications
    ···› USA

0590 ···› Mixer
    ···› Switzerland

0591 ···› Warm Rain Ltd
    ···› UK

0592 ···› Warm Rain Ltd
    ···› UK

0594 ⟶ **Let Her Press**
⟶ USA

0595 ⟶ **On The Edge Design, Inc**
⟶ USA

0596 ⋯→ The Levy Restaurants
⋯→ USA

0597 ⋯→ Disney Design Group
⋯→ USA

0598 ⋯→ Jeff Fisher LogoMotives
⋯→ USA

0599 ⋯→ Associates Design
⋯→ USA

0600 ---> Smart Works
  ---> Australia

0601 ---> Val Gene Associates
  ---> USA

0602 ---> The Levy Restaurants
  ---> USA

0603 ---> Adrienne Weiss Corporation
  ---> USA

THE OFFICIAL MENU FOR FAMISHED FANS

PIZZA
A 10-inch pizza, baked fresh and hot with your choice of ham, beef or pepperoni topping. All include onions, mushrooms, bell pepper and jalapeno peppers.
$8.20

BURGERS
Six ounces of fresh ground beef, charbroiled and served dressed on a toasted bun. Served with fries.
$5.95   **with cheese $6.60**

POBOYS
Your choice of ham, roast beef or turkey on freshly-baked French bread with lettuce, tomato, red onion and pickles. Your choice of chips or fries.
$5.95

HOT DOG
A large, all-beef hot dog on Louisiana French bread covered with chili, cheese and onions. Served with fries.
$4.95

CHIPOTLE CHICKEN TENDERS
A half-pound of tender chicken, fried to perfection and served with blue cheese or ranch dipping sauce. Served with fries.
$5.95

NACHOS
Crisp chips covered with chili, cheese and jalapenos.
$3.45

WINGS
Wings, grilled or fried, served either mild or hot, with ranch dressing and celery sticks.
10 wings $6.95   20 wings $9.95

CHEESE FRIES
Heaps of freshly-cooked fries served with melted cheddar cheese and jalapenos.
$2.95

CHIPS & SALSA

THE OFFICIAL MENU FOR FAMISHED FANS

PIZZA
A 10-inch pizza, baked fresh and hot with your choice of ham, beef or pepperoni topping. All include onions, mushrooms, bell pepper and jalapeno peppers.
$8.20

BURGERS
Six ounces of fresh ground beef, charbroiled and served dressed on a toasted bun. Served with fries.
$5.95   **with cheese $6.60**

POBOYS
Your choice of ham, roast beef or turkey on freshly-baked French bread with lettuce, tomato, red onion and pickles. Your choice of chips or fries.
$5.95

HOT DOG
A large, all-beef hot dog on Louisiana French bread covered with chili, cheese and onions. Served with fries.
$4.95

CHIPOTLE CHICKEN TENDERS
A half-pound of tender chicken, fried to perfection and served with blue cheese or ranch dipping sauce. Served with fries.
$5.95

NACHOS
Crisp chips covered with chili, cheese and jalapenos.
$3.45

WINGS
Wings, grilled or fried, served either mild or hot, with ranch dressing and celery sticks.
10 wings $6.95   20 wings $9.95

CHEESE FRIES
Heaps of freshly-cooked fries served with melted cheddar cheese and jalapenos.
$2.95

CHIPS & SALSA

THE OFFICIAL MENU
FOR FAMISHED FANS

PIZZA
A 10-inch pizza, baked fresh and hot with your choice of ham, beef or pepperoni topping. All include onions, mushrooms, bell pepper and jalapeno peppers.
$8.20

BURGERS
Six ounces of fresh ground beef, charbroiled and served dressed on a toasted bun. Served with fries.
$5.95   **with cheese $6.60**

POBOYS
Your choice of ham, roast beef or turkey on freshly-baked French bread with lettuce, tomato, red onion and pickles. Your choice of chips or fries.
$5.95

HOT DOG
A large, all-beef hot dog on Louisiana French bread covered with chili, cheese and onions. Served with fries.
$4.95

CHIPOTLE CHICKEN TENDERS
A half-pound of tender chicken, fried to perfection and served with blue cheese or ranch dipping sauce. Served with fries.
$5.95

NACHOS
Crisp chips covered with chili, cheese and jalapenos.
$3.45

WINGS
Wings, grilled or fried, served either mild or hot, with ranch dressing and celery sticks.
10 wings $6.95   20 wings $9.95

CHEESE FRIES
Heaps of freshly-cooked fries served with melted cheddar cheese and jalapenos.
$2.95

CHIPS & SALSA

THE OFFICIAL MENU
FOR FAMISHED FANS

PIZZA
A 10-inch pizza, baked fresh and hot with your choice of ham, beef or pepperoni topping. All include onions, mushrooms, bell pepper and jalapeno peppers.
$8.20

BURGERS
Six ounces of fresh ground beef, charbroiled and served dressed on a toasted bun. Served with fries.
$5.95   **with cheese $6.60**

POBOYS
Your choice of ham, roast beef or turkey on freshly-baked French bread with lettuce, tomato, red onion and pickles. Your choice of chips or fries.
$5.95

HOT DOG
A large, all-beef hot dog on Louisiana French bread covered with chili, cheese and onions. Served with fries.
$4.95

CHIPOTLE CHICKEN TENDERS
A half-pound of tender chicken, fried to perfection and served with blue cheese or ranch dipping sauce. Served with fries.
$5.95

NACHOS
Crisp chips covered with chili, cheese and jalapenos.
$3.45

WINGS
Wings, grilled or fried, served either mild or hot, with ranch dressing and celery sticks.
10 wings $6.95   20 wings $9.95

CHEESE FRIES
Heaps of freshly-cooked fries served with melted cheddar cheese and jalapenos.
$2.95

CHIPS & SALSA

0608 ⋯➔ Disney Design Group
⋯➔ USA

0609 ⋯➔ Disney Design Group
⋯➔ USA

0610 ⋯➔ PPA Design Limited
⋯➔ Hong Kong

0611 ⋯➔ PPA Design Limited
⋯➔ Hong Kong

0612 ···› Raven Madd Design Company
···› New Zealand

0614 ⇢ Dean Johnson Design
⇢ USA

0615 ⇢ John Evans Design
⇢ USA

0616 ⇢ Whitney-Edwards Design
⇢ USA

0617 ⇢ Disney Design Group
⇢ USA

0618 ⋯⇢ S&N Design
⋯⇢ USA

0620 ⇢ Pentagram Design
⇢ USA

0621 ⇢ Pentagram Design
⇢ USA

0622 ⇢ S&N Design
⇢ USA

0623 ⇢ Fabrice Praeger
⇢ France

0624 → Associates Design
→ USA

0625 → Associates Design
→ USA

0626 → Associates Design
→ USA

0627 → Annabelle Wimer Design
→ USA

0628 ⟶ PPA Design Limited
⟶ Hong Kong

0629 ⟶ Gloria Paul
⟶ USA

0630 ⟶ Associates Design
⟶ USA

0631 ⟶ Associates Design
⟶ USA

0633 ⟶ Sayles Graphic Design
⟶ USA

0634 ⟶ The Levy Restaurants
⟶ USA

0635 ⟶ Schumaker
⟶ USA

0636 ⟶ The Levy Restaurants
⟶ USA

0637 ⇢ Corbin Design
   ⇢ USA

0638 ⇢ Richard Poulin Design Group
   ⇢ USA

0639 ⇢ PM Design
   ⇢ USA

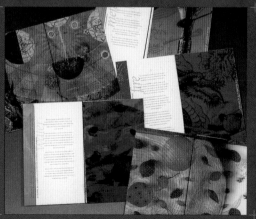

0640 ⇢ PPA Design Limited
   ⇢ Hong Kong

0641 ⇢ XJR Design
⇢ USA

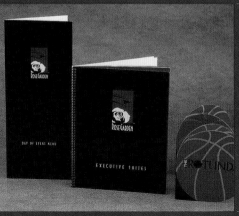

0642 ⇢ David Carter Design
⇢ USA

0643 ⇢ Sabin Design
⇢ USA

0644 ⇢ The Levy Restaurants
⇢ USA

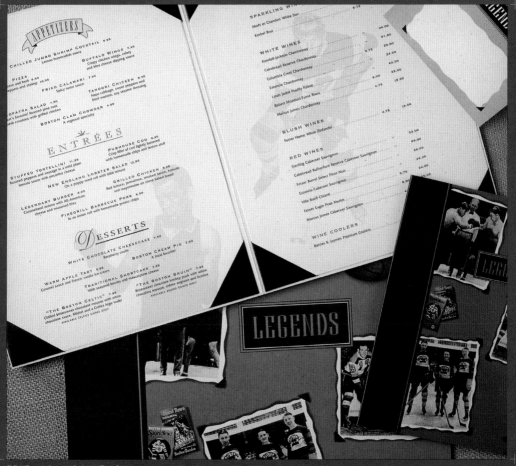

APPETIZERS

CHILLED JUMBO SHRIMP COCKTAIL 9.95
Lemon horseradish sauce

BUFFALO WINGS 7.25
Crispy chicken wings, celery
and bleu cheese dipping sauce

PIZZA
cheese and herb 8.50
peppers and shrimp 10.95

FRIED CALAMARI 7.95
Spicy tartar sauce

TANDORI CHICKEN 8.95
Napa cabbage, sweet peppers and
fried wonton, soy sesame dressing

OPATRA SALAD 7.50
's favorite! Roasted pine nuts
rb croutons with grilled chicken

BOSTON CLAM CHOWDER 4.95
A regional specialty

ENTRÉES

PUSHHOUSE COD 9.95
Crisp fillet of cod lightly battered
with homemade chips and lemon shell

STUFFED TORTELLINI 11.95
Roasted peppers and sausage in a mild plum
tomato sauce with pecorino cheese

NEW ENGLAND LOBSTER SALAD 12.95
On a poppy seed roll with bibb lettuce

GRILLED CHICKEN 8.95
Red lettuce, provolone, smoked bacon, tomato
and mayonnaise on stone baked bread

LEGENDARY BURGER 8.95
Caramelized onions with All-American
cheese and seasoned fries

FIREGRILL BARBECUE PORK 9.50
In an onion roll with homemade potato chips

DESSERTS

WHITE CHOCOLATE CHEESECAKE 7.50
Raspberry coulis

BOSTON CREAM PIE 7.00
A local favorite!

WARM APPLE TART 6.95
Caramel sauce and French vanilla ice cream

TRADITIONAL SHORTCAKE 7.25
With seasonal berries and mascarpone cheese

"THE BOSTON BRUIN" 7.95
Bittersweet chocolate puck with white
chocolate mousse, crème anglaise and licorice
AVAILABLE BRUINS GAMES ONLY

"THE BOSTON CELTIC" 7.95
Clotted bittersweet chocolate mousse with white
chocolate sauce, Midori and a Celtics logo wafer
AVAILABLE CELTICS GAMES ONLY

SPARKLING WINE 8.75

Moët et Chandon White Star 30.00
Korbel Brut 61.00

WHITE WINES

Kendall-Jackson Chardonnay 6.75 34.00
Cakebread Reserve Chardonnay 49.00
Columbia Crest Chardonnay 6.00 28.00
Estancia Chardonnay 4.75 19.00
Louis Jadot Pouilly Fuissé
Robert Mondavi Fume Blanc
Marcus James Chardonnay 4.75 19.00

BLUSH WINES

Sutter Home White Zinfandel 33.00

RED WINES

Sterling Cabernet Sauvignon 69.00
Cakebread Rutherford Reserve Cabernet Sauvignon 26.00
Fetzer Barrel Select Pinot Noir 26.00
Estancia Cabernet Sauvignon 5.75 34.00
Villa Batil Chianti 25.00
Fetzer Eagle Peak Merlot
Marcus James Cabernet Sauvignon

WINE COOLERS

Bartles & Jaymes Premium Coolers

0647 ---> Adventure Advertising
   ---> USA

0648 ---> Richard Poulin Design Group
   ---> USA

0649 ---> Sayles Graphic Design
   ---> USA

0650 ---> On The Edge Design, Inc
   ---> USA

0651 ⋯⟩ Associates Design
⋯⟩ USA

0652 ⋯⟩ Mind's Eye Studio
⋯⟩ Canada

0653 ⋯⟩ Eilts Anderson Tracy
⋯⟩ USA

0654 ⋯⟩ Mind's Eye Studio
⋯⟩ Canada

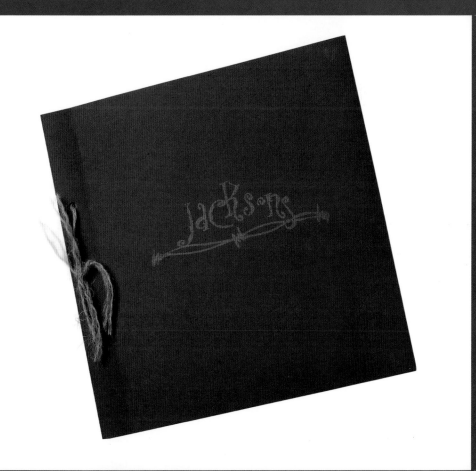

0656 ⇢ Raidy Printing Group SAL
⇢ Lebanon

0657 ⇢ AdamsMorioka
⇢ USA

0658 ‑‑‑> Bullet Communications Inc
   ‑‑‑> USA

0659 ‑‑‑> DZ6 Design
   ‑‑‑> Brazil

0660 ‑‑‑> Associates Design
   ‑‑‑> USA

0661 ‑‑‑> Rusty Kay & Associates
   ‑‑‑> USA

0662 ⇢ McCord Graphic Design
⇢ Country unavailable

0663 ⇢ Bright & Associates
⇢ USA

0664 ⇢ Associates Design
⇢ USA

0665 ⇢ Shamlian Advertising
⇢ USA

0666 ⋯→ **Emma Main**
⋯→ New Zealand

0667 ⋯→ **Marve Cooper Design, Ltd.**
⋯→ USA

0668 ⋯→ **PPA Design Limited**
⋯→ Hong Kong

0669 ⋯→ **PPA Design Limited**
⋯→ Hong Kong

0670–0728

04

CHAPTER 4
PACKAGING

BAGS
BOXES
CARTONS
BOTTLES
WRAPPERS

0671 ⟶ Inaria
⟶ UK

0672 ⟶ Hornall Anderson Design Works
⟶ USA

0673 ⟶ LM
⟶ UK

0674 ⟶ CDI Studios
⟶ USA

0675 ⇢ David Caunce
⇢ UK

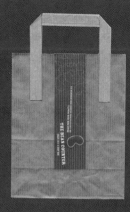

0676 ⇢ David Caunce
⇢ UK

0677 ⇢ David Caunce
⇢ UK

0678 ⇢ Warm Rain Ltd
⇢ UK

0682 ···> Artie Horowitz Design
···> USA

0683 ···> R&Mag Graphic Design
···> Italy

0684 ···> Public
···> USA

0685 ···> Bullet Communications Inc
···> USA

0686 ···> bonbon london
    ···> UK

0687 ···> bonbon london
    ···> UK

0688 ···> bonbon london
    ···> UK

0689 ···> bonbon london
    ···> UK

0690 ⋯⟶ Inaria
     ⋯⟶ UK

0691 ⋯⟶ Warm Rain Ltd
     ⋯⟶ UK

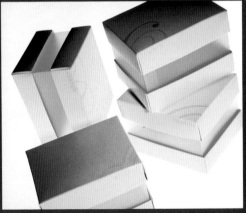

0692 ⋯⟶ Warm Rain Ltd
     ⋯⟶ UK

0693 ⋯⟶ Warm Rain Ltd
     ⋯⟶ UK

0695 ⋯⋑ Willoughby Design Group
⋯⋑ USA

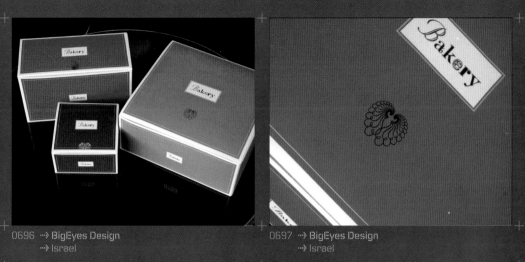

0696 ⋯⋟ BigEyes Design
⋯⋟ Israel

0697 ⋯⋟ BigEyes Design
⋯⋟ Israel

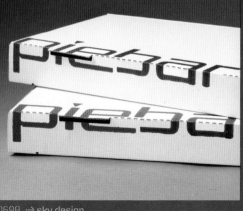

0698 ⋯⋟ sky design
⋯⋟ USA

0699 ⋯⋟ sky design
⋯⋟ USA

0702 ⇢ David Caunce
⇢ UK

0703 ⇢ David Caunce
⇢ UK

0704 ⇢ Hornall Anderson Design Works
⇢ USA

0705 ⇢ Rome & Gold Creative
⇢ USA

0706 ⤏ Willoughby Design Group
⤏ USA

0707 ⤏ BigEyes Design
⤏ Israel

0708 ⤏ Rome & Gold Creative
⤏ USA

0709 ⤏ Rome & Gold Creative
⤏ USA

0710 ⋯⇢ Vrontikis Design Office
      ⋯⇢ USA

0711 ---> Hornall Anderson Design Works
      ---> USA

0712 ---> Hornall Anderson Design Works
      ---> USA

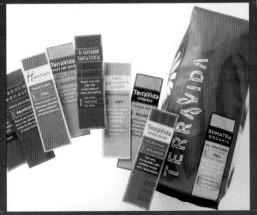

0713 ---> Hornall Anderson Design Works
      ---> USA

0714 ---> Evenson Design Group
      ---> USA

0715 ⤏ urban INFLUENCE design studio
⤏ USA

0717 ⟶ bonbon london
⟶ UK

0718 ⋯⋯ Regan Blough
⋯⋯ USA

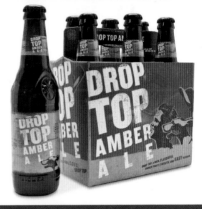

0719 ⋯⋯ Hornall Anderson Design Works
⋯⋯ USA

0720 ⋯⋯ Hornall Anderson Design Works
⋯⋯ USA

0721 ⋯⋯ Hornall Anderson Design Works
⋯⋯ USA

0722 ⇢ Hans Flink Design Inc.
⇢ USA

0723 ⇢ Hans Flink Design Inc.
⇢ USA

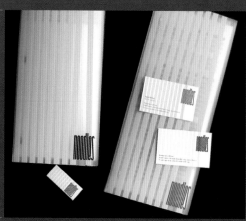

0724 ⇢ Mimolimit
⇢ Czech Republic

0725 ⇢ Bright & Associates
⇢ USA

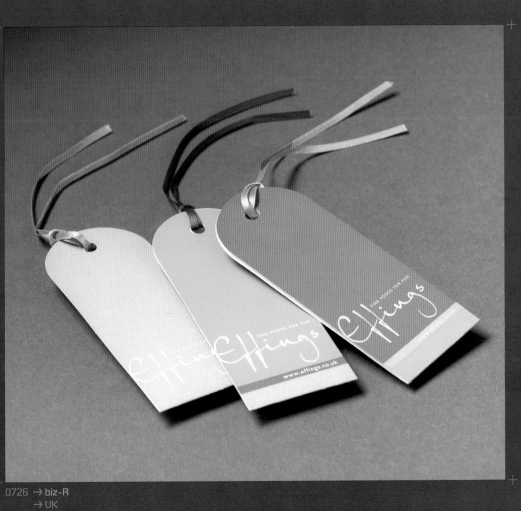

0728 ⋯⋗ Vrontikis Design Office
⋯⋗ USA

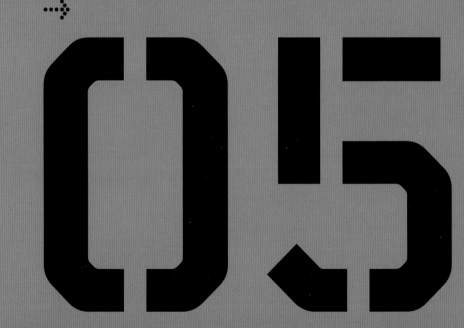

0729-0896 →

05

CHAPTER 5
PROMOTIONAL ITEMS

0730 ⇢ Mirko Ilić Corp.
⇢ USA

0731 ⇢ Graphic Content
⇢ USA

0732 ⇢ Inaria
⇢ UK

0733 ⇢ Warm Rain Ltd
⇢ UK

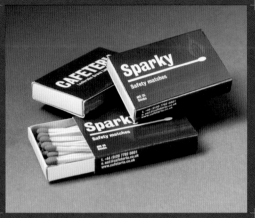

0734 ⋯→ bonbon london
⋯→ UK

0735 ⋯→ 804© Graphic Design
⋯→ Germany

0736 ⋯→ Regan Blough
⋯→ USA

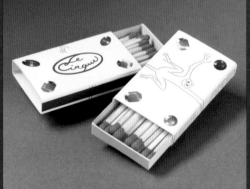

0737 ⋯→ Mirko Ilić Corp.
⋯→ USA

0738 ⋯→ From Scratch Design Studio
⋯→ USA

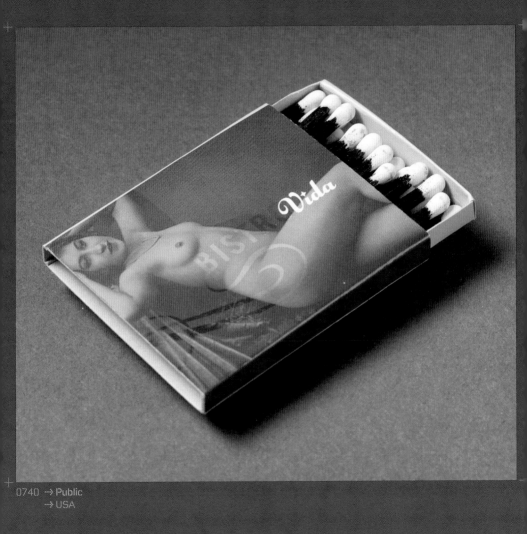

0741 ⟶ Ducks Design
⟶ Germany

0742 ⟶ Louise Fili Ltd.
⟶ USA

0743 ⟶ Pentagram Design
⟶ USA

0744 ⟶ Vrontikis Design Office
⟶ USA

0745 ⋯⇢ i_d buero
⋯⇢ Germany

0746 ⋯⇢ Turnstyle
⋯⇢ USA

0747 ⋯⇢ Northern Artisan
⋯⇢ USA

0748 ⋯⇢ CWA Inc.
⋯⇢ USA

0749 ⇢ AdamsMorioka
⇢ USA

0750 ⇢ AdamsMorioka
⇢ USA

0751 ⇢ Finest/Magma
⇢ Germany

0752 ⇢ Finest/Magma
⇢ Germany

0753 --> TD2, Identity & Strategic Design
--> Mexico

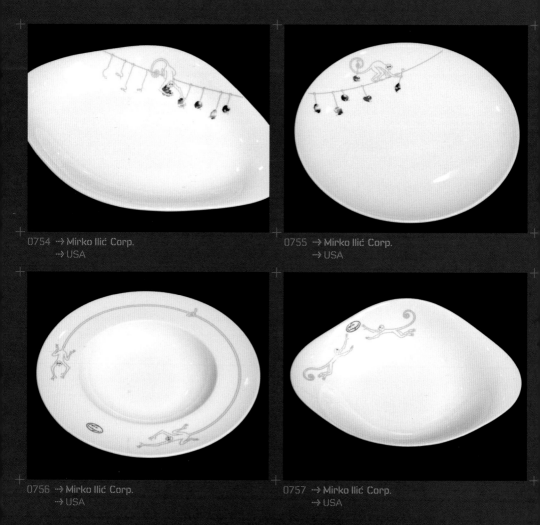

0754 ⋯⇢ Mirko Ilić Corp.
⋯⇢ USA

0755 ⋯⇢ Mirko Ilić Corp.
⋯⇢ USA

0756 ⋯⇢ Mirko Ilić Corp.
⋯⇢ USA

0757 ⋯⇢ Mirko Ilić Corp.
⋯⇢ USA

0758 ⋯⋗ Mirko Ilić Corp.
    ⋯⋗ USA

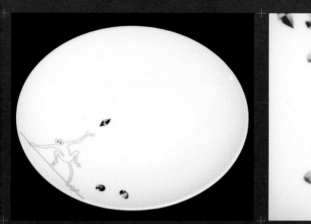

0760 ···> Mirko Ilić Corp.
   ···> USA

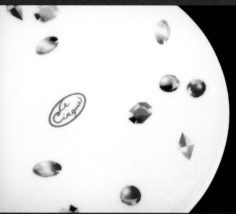

0761 ···> Mirko Ilić Corp.
   ···> USA

0762 ···> Mirko Ilić Corp.
   ···> USA

0763 ···> Mirko Ilić Corp.
   ···> USA

MARCI BREITLING & BOB FINLAYSON
INVITE YOU TO CELEBRATE
THE V.I.P. GRAND OPENING OF

TASTINGS

A new concept in fine food and wine

THURSDAY, OCTOBER 20, 2005
6:30 IN THE EVENING

ATRIUM AT 69930 HIGHWAY 111
NCHO MIRAGE, CALIFORNIA

SE R.S.V.P. JANET NEWCOMB
200.8684 BY OCTOBER 15

COCKTAIL ATTIRE

T

TASTINGS

0764 ⇢ Chris Rooney
⇢ USA

0765 ⋯→ **Mirko Ilić Corp.**
⋯→ USA

0766 ⋯→ **Mimolimit**
⋯→ Czech Republic

0767 ⋯→ **Mimolimit**
⋯→ Czech Republic

0768 ⋯→ **Rome & Gold Creative**
⋯→ USA

0770 ⇢ 804© Graphic Design
⇢ Germany

0771 ⇢ Nita B. Creative
⇢ USA

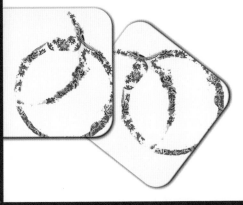

0772 ⇢ Brandhouse WTS
⇢ UK

0773 ⇢ Finest/Magma
⇢ Germany

0774 ⇢ bonbon london
    ⇢ UK

0775 ⇢ On The Edge Design, Inc
    ⇢ USA

0776 ⇢ Ultra Design
    ⇢ USA

0777 ⇢ Hollis Brand Communications
    ⇢ USA

0778 ⤳ **Hollis Brand Communications**
⤳ USA

0779 ⟶ On The Edge Design, Inc
⟶ USA

0780 ⟶ On The Edge Design, Inc
⟶ USA

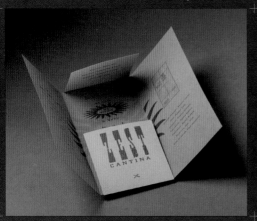

0781 ⟶ Vrontikis Design Office
⟶ USA

0782 ⟶ Braue Strategic Brand Design
⟶ Germany

0785 ...⇢ **Dornig Graphic Design**
...⇢ Austria

0786 ...⇢ **Warm Rain Ltd**
...⇢ UK

0787 ...⇢ **Hollis Brand Communications**
...⇢ USA

0788 ...⇢ **biz-R**
...⇢ UK

CAF53AR

CAF53AR FÜNFDREI
AMALIENSTRASSE 53 76133 KARLSRUHE
WWW.FUENFDREI.DE

TREU530NUS

ab zehn mal fünfdrei
gibt es ein getränk bis 5,30 € umsonst!

AFTERWORK.START
MITTWOCHS
18-21 UHR
CAFEBAR FÜNFDREI **53**

SNACKS GRATIS
UND FREIER EINTRITT IM E-CLUB

AB 19.10.2005

0789 ⇢ Finest/Magma
⇢ Germany

0790 ⇢ Finest/Magma
⇢ Germany

0791 ⇢ Finest/Magma
⇢ Germany

0792 ⇢ Hollis Brand Communications
⇢ USA

0795 ⋯→ bonbon london
   ⋯→ UK

0796 ⋯→ bonbon london
   ⋯→ UK

0797 ⋯→ On The Edge Design, Inc
   ⋯→ USA

0798 ⋯→ On The Edge Design, Inc
   ⋯→ USA

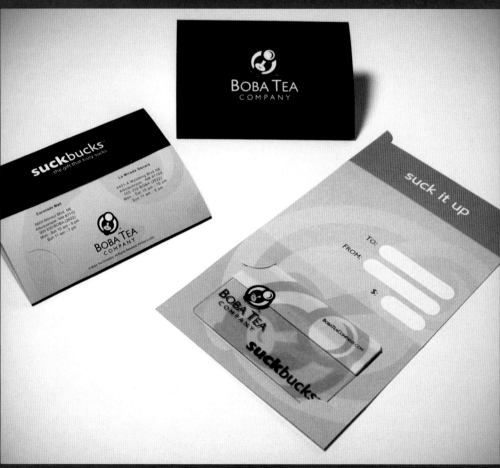

David Wilhelm's Culinary Adventures Presents...

CHAT NOIR

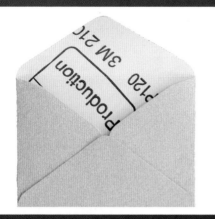

0801 ⇢ Warm Rain Ltd
⇢ UK

0802 ⇢ Crush Design & Art Direction
⇢ UK

0803 ⇢ Hollis Brand Communications
⇢ USA

0804 ⇢ BigEyes Design
⇢ Israel

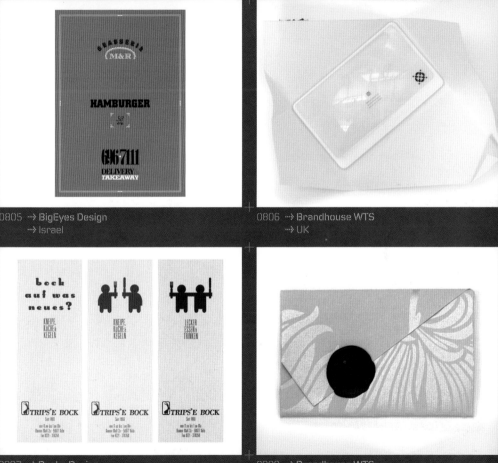

0805 --> BigEyes Design
--> Israel

0806 --> Brandhouse WTS
--> UK

0807 --> Ducks Design
--> Germany

0808 --> Brandhouse WTS
--> UK

0810 ⇢ Brandhouse WTS
    ⇢ UK

0811 ⇢ R&Mag Graphic Design
    ⇢ Italy

0812 ⇢ Frost Design, Sydney
    ⇢ Australia

0813 ⇢ Fresh Oil
    ⇢ USA

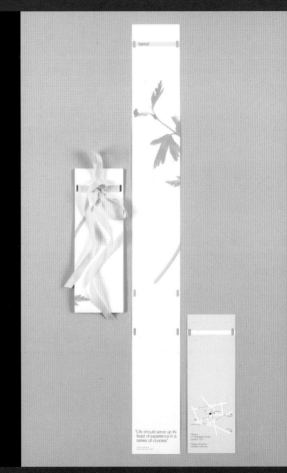

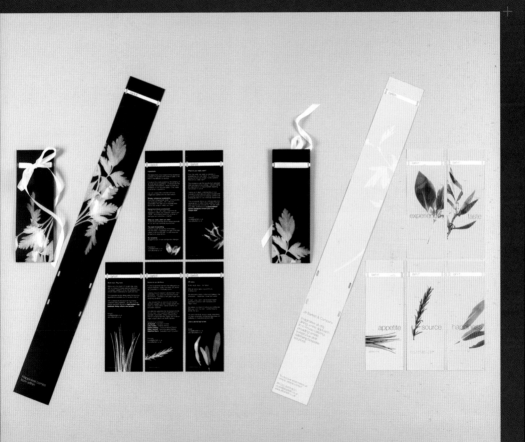

CATCH the CARAMEL Karma

Caramel Wowieccino
Rich espresso & caramel blended
with ice & vanilla custard
small 3.30 medium 3.80 large 4.30

Sheridan's
LATTÉS

Top off Your Morn!

Irish Vanilla Latté
Espresso, Irish cream syrup steamed with
Sheridan's vanilla custard
small 3.25 medium 3.80 large 4.10

Sheridan's
LATTÉS

What a lovely BUNCH

Honey-Nana-Nut Wowieccino
Rich espresso, bananas, peanut butter &
honey blended with ice & vanilla custard,
topped with whipped cream
small 3.40 medium 4.00 large 4.60

Sheridan's
LATTÉS

TWO nuts WALK into a chocolate bar...

Choco-Nut Latté
Rich espresso, hazelnut syrup, almond syrup
& steamed chocolate milk.
small 3.25 medium 3.80 large 4.10

Sheridan's
LATTÉS

0816 ⟶ Willoughby Design Group
⟶ USA

0817 ⟶ Willoughby Design Group
⟶ USA

La tartine

0818 ⟶ Hand Made Group
⟶ Italy

bardimartino

ENOTECA • CAFFETTERIA • DOLCI TIPICI

SAL DE RISO

0819 ⟶ R&Mag Graphic Design
⟶ Italy

hacienda

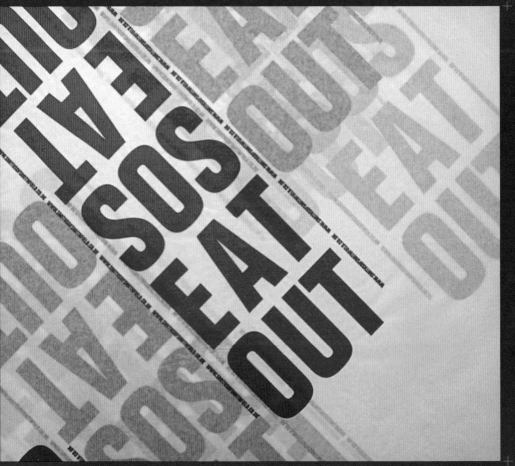

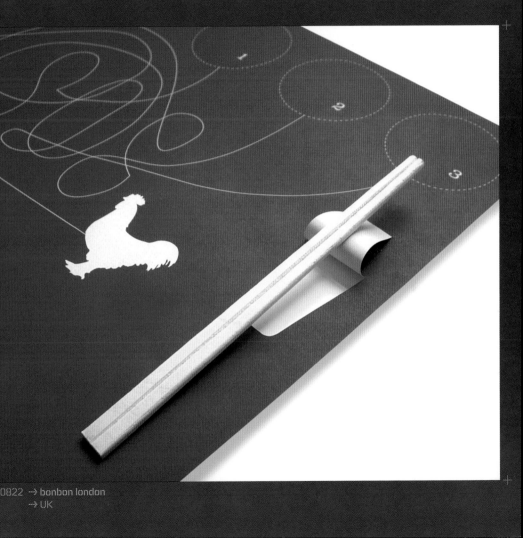

0822 ⋯⋯➤ bonbon london
⋯⋯➤ UK

0824 ⋯➤ Turnstyle
⋯➤ USA

0825 ⋯➤ Vrontikis Design Office
⋯➤ USA

0826 ⋯➤ Fresh Oil
⋯➤ USA

0827 ⋯➤ David Caunce
⋯➤ UK

0828 ⇢ **Hollis Brand Communications**
⇢ USA

0829 ⇢ **R&Mag Graphic Design**
⇢ Italy

0830 ⇢ **Fullblastinc.com**
⇢ USA

0831 ⇢ **Braue Strategic Brand Design**
⇢ Germany

0833 ⟶ **Smart Works**
⟶ Australia

SAUCY TUNES

upstairs in the cocktail bar, with DJ's on Thursday, Friday & Saturday evenings...

CAFETERIA
Ladbroke Grove London W10

armlessdragon

0834 ⇢ bonbon london
⇢ UK

0835 ⇢ Elfen
⇢ Wales

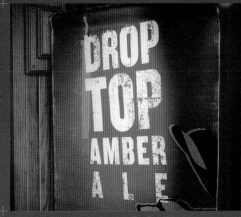

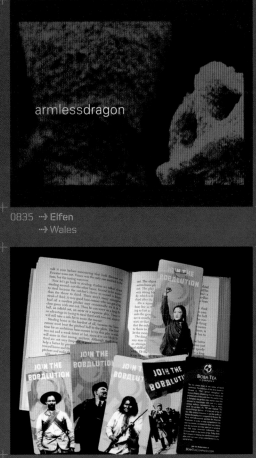

0836 ⇢ Hornall Anderson Design Works
⇢ USA

0837 ⇢ Rome & Gold Creative
⇢ USA

0838 ⋯→ Rome & Gold Creative
⋯→ USA

0839 ⋯→ Rome & Gold Creative
⋯→ USA

0840 ⋯→ Rome & Gold Creative
⋯→ USA

0841 ⋯→ Rome & Gold Creative
⋯→ USA

Von nun an   schwingt der Sohn die Kelle!

partake in the parlour at sketch monday to thursday's from 20th june to
the end of august 2005 and receive 10% off your final bill

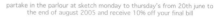

0843 ···> Warm Rain Ltd
       ···> UK

0844 ···> Warm Rain Ltd
       ···> UK

0845 ···> Warm Rain Ltd
       ···> UK

0846 ···> Warm Rain Ltd
       ···> UK

0847 ⋯→ Warm Rain Ltd
⋯→ UK

0848 ⋯→ Warm Rain Ltd
⋯→ UK

0849 ⋯→ Northern Artisan
⋯→ USA

0850 ⋯→ Bartosz Oczujda
⋯→ Poland

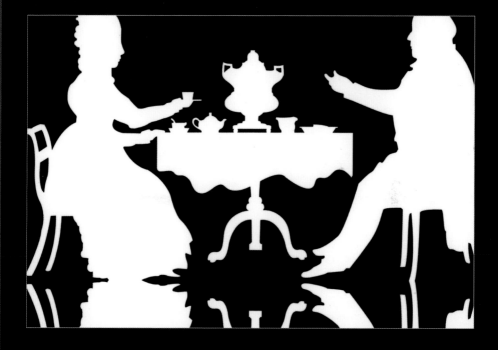

0853 ⇢ Hornall Anderson Design Works
⇢ USA

0854 ⇢ Hornall Anderson Design Works
⇢ USA

0855 ⇢ Hornall Anderson Design Works
⇢ USA

0856 ⇢ Hornall Anderson Design Works
⇢ USA

0857 ···▸ Threefold
···▸ Australia

0858 ···▸ Spark Studio Pty Ltd
···▸ Australia

0859 ···▸ BASELINE
···▸ Scotland

0860 ···▸ Laura Jacoby
···▸ USA

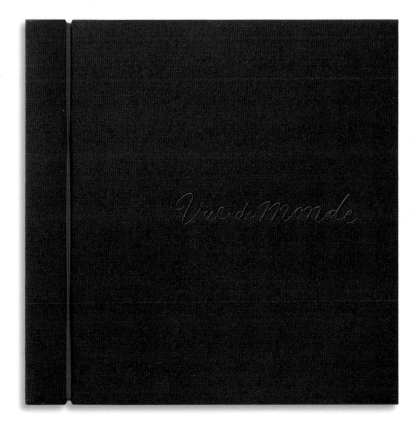

0863 ⋯→ bonbon london
⋯→ UK

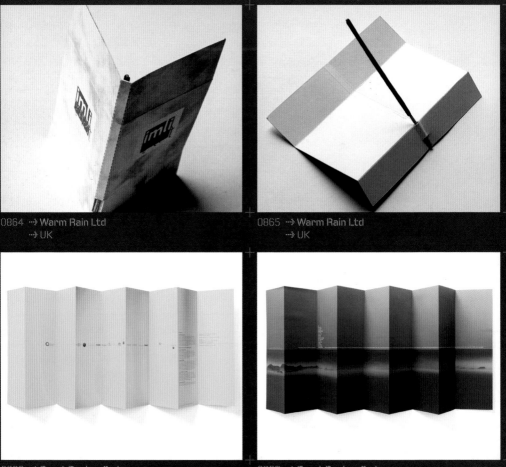

0864 ⋯→ Warm Rain Ltd
⋯→ UK

0865 ⋯→ Warm Rain Ltd
⋯→ UK

0866 ⋯→ Frost Design, Sydney

0867 ⋯→ Frost Design, Sydney

0868 ···⟩ **Frost Design, Sydney**
···⟩ Australia

0869 ···⟩ **Smart Works**
···⟩ Australia

0870 ···⟩ **Vrontikis Design Office**
···⟩ USA

0871 ···⟩ **Ducks Design**
···⟩ Germany

0873 ⋯⋙ Rome & Gold Creative
⋯⋙ USA

0874 ⋯⋙ Rome & Gold Creative
⋯⋙ USA

0875 ⋯⋙ Evenson Design Group
⋯⋙ USA

0876 ⋯⋙ CDI Studios
⋯⋙ USA

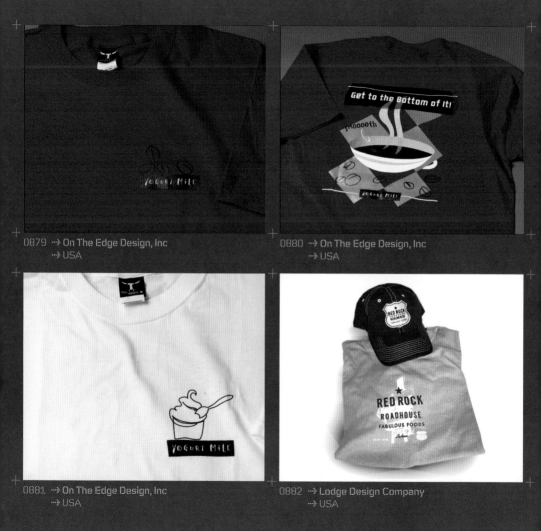

0879 ┈→ On The Edge Design, Inc
┈→ USA

0880 ┈→ On The Edge Design, Inc
┈→ USA

0881 ┈→ On The Edge Design, Inc
┈→ USA

0882 ┈→ Lodge Design Company
┈→ USA

0883 ⋯→ Campus Collection
      ⋯→ USA

0884 ⋯→ Campus Collection
      ⋯→ USA

0885 ⋯→ Campus Collection
      ⋯→ USA

0886 ⋯→ Fullblastinc.com
      ⋯→ USA

0887 ⋯⇥ Campus Collection
⋯⇥ USA

0888 ⋯⇥ Campus Collection
⋯⇥ USA

0889 ⋯⇥ Campus Collection
⋯⇥ USA

0890 ⋯⇥ Campus Collection
⋯⇥ USA

0893 --→ On The Edge Design, Inc
--→ USA

0894 --→ On The Edge Design, Inc
--→ USA

0895 --→ On The Edge Design, Inc
--→ USA

0896 --→ Sagmeister Inc
--→ USA

06

0897-1.0000 →

0680

CHAPTER 6
STATIONERY

BUSINESS CARDS
LETTERHEAD
FOLDERS
ENVELOPES

0898 ···> i_d buero
···> Germany

0899 ···> i_d buero
···> Germany

0900 ···> Fabrice Praeger
···> France

0901 ···> 804© Graphic Design
···> Germany

0902 ⇢ christiansen: creative
  ⇢ USA

0903 ⇢ Public
  ⇢ USA

0904 ⇢ Public
  ⇢ USA

0905 ⇢ bonbon london
  ⇢ UK

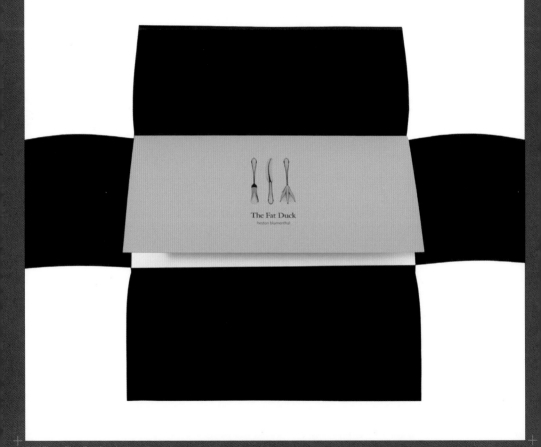

The Fat Duck
heston blumenthal

Heston Blumenthal

0909 ···> i_d buero
···> Germany

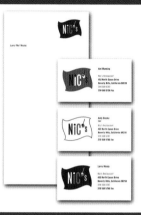

0910 ···> AdamsMorioka
···> USA

0911 ···> Smart Works
···> Australia

0912 ···> Fabrice Praeger
···> France

091.3 --> Spark Studio Pty Ltd
--> Australia

091.4 --> DZ6 Design
--> Brazil

091.5 --> Bakken Creative Company
--> USA

091.6 --> Bakken Creative Company
--> USA

0917 ⇢ Turnstyle
⇢ USA

0918 ⇢ Frost Design, Sydney
⇢ Australia

0919 ⇢ Frost Design, Sydney
⇢ Australia

0920 ⇢ Frost Design, Sydney
⇢ Australia

SMELLING MISTAKE.

WINE MAKES YOU HAPPY.

Vue de Monde

VUE DE MONDE · NORMANBY CHAMBERS
430 LITTLE COLLINS ST MELBOURNE VIC 3000
TELEPHONE 03 9691 3888 FACSIMILE 03 9600 4600
vuedemonde@vuedemonde.com.au and www.vuedemonde.com.au

0921 ⋯⋗ Threefold
⋯⋗ Australia

0923 --> Hardy Design
--> Brazil

0924 --> On The Edge Design, Inc
--> USA

0925 --> On The Edge Design, Inc
--> USA

0926 --> On The Edge Design, Inc
--> USA

0927 ⋯⇢ bonbon london
⋯⇢ UK

0928 ⋯⇢ bonbon london
⋯⇢ UK

0929 ⋯⇢ urban INFLUENCE design studio
⋯⇢ USA

0930 ⋯⇢ urban INFLUENCE design studio
⋯⇢ USA

LOUISA MOUELLEF
Guest Relations

Direct tel:
Fax:
Mobile: +44(0)870 770 65 26
               +44(0)207 629 16 84
               +44(0)777 573 75 33

loulsam@sketch.uk.com

Sketch 9 Conduit Street London W1S 2XG
www.sketch.uk.com

Guest r

Direct tel: +44(0)2
Fax:
Mobile: +44(0)777 573

loulsam@sketch.uk.com

Sketch 9 Conduit Street London W1S 2XG
www.sketch.uk.com

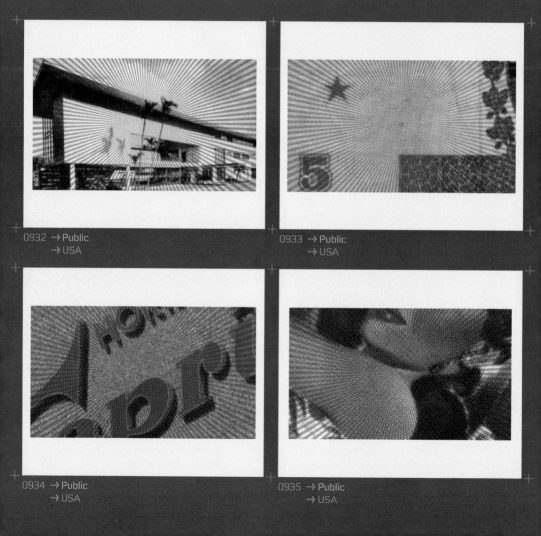

0932 ⇢ Public
⇢ USA

0933 ⇢ Public
⇢ USA

0934 ⇢ Public
⇢ USA

0935 ⇢ Public
⇢ USA

'Smiths' of Smithfield
Outside Catering

SOS
OUT

Paul Robinson–Webster

67-77 Charterhouse Street London EC1M 6HJ
Tel: 020 7251 7955 Fax: 020 7236 0488
E-Mail: paul@smithsofsmithfield.co.uk
www.smithsofsmithfield.co.uk

0937 ...⟩ bonbon london
...⟩ UK

cafe LO CUBANO
—— COFFEE BAR ——

THOMAS POST :: tpost@cafelocubano.com

527 Howard Street :: 4th Floor :: San Francisco :: California :: 94105
t : 415 371 9933 :: f : 415 371 9955
www.cafelocubano.com

0938 ...⟩ Public
...⟩ USA

0939 ...⟩ bonbon london
...⟩ UK

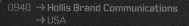

A.J. Voytko

558 fourth avenue san diego ca 92101
call 619.232.4483 fax 619.232.4489
www.chiverestaurant.com

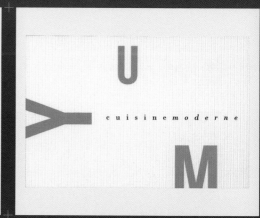

0940 ⟶ Hollis Brand Communications
     ⟶ USA

0941 ⟶ Hollis Brand Communications
     ⟶ USA

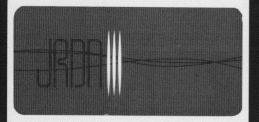

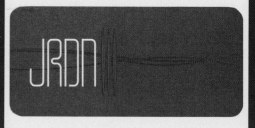

0942 ⟶ Hollis Brand Communications
     ⟶ USA

0943 ⟶ Hollis Brand Communications
     ⟶ USA

bezu

FRENCH-ASIAN CUISINE

9812 Falls Rd.
POTOMAC Md, 20854
TEL.: 301.299.3000
FAX: 301.299.3102
WWW.BEZURESTAURANT.COM
CONTACT@BEZURESTAURANT.COM

12

Café-Restaurant
Ouvert tous les jours
102 rue St-Honoré, Paris 1er
Téléphone : 01 53 40 76 22

= *La Petite Epicerie*

0946 ⇢ Fabrice Praeger
⇢ France

12

Café-Restaurant
Ouvert tous les jours
102 rue St-Honoré, Paris 1er
Téléphone : 01 53 40 76 22

= *La Petite Epicerie*

0947 ⇢ Fabrice Praeger
⇢ France

12

Café-Restaurant
Ouvert tous les jours
102 rue St-Honoré, Paris 1er
Téléphone : 01 53 40 76 22

= *La Petite Epicerie*

0948 ⇢ Fabrice Praeger
⇢ France

Great Coffee   *Great Music*

MILKBOY
COFFEE

2 EAST LANCASTER AVENUE ARDMORE, PA 19003
TEL (610) 645-5269 | FAX (610) 645-5329
WEB WWW.MILKBOYCOFFEE.COM | EMAIL INFO@

0949 ⇢ Bowhaus Design Groupe
⇢ USA

0950 ⋯→ **Ayse Çelem**
⋯→ Turkey

0951 ⋯→ **bonbon london**
⋯→ UK

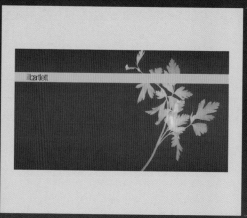

0952 ⋯→ **bonbon london**
⋯→ UK

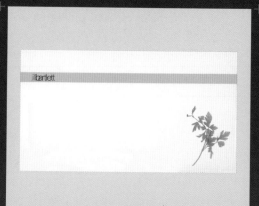

0953 ⋯→ **bonbon london**
⋯→ UK

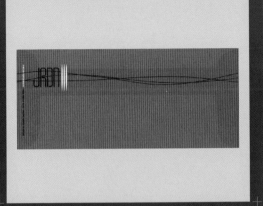

0954 ┈┈> **Hollis Brand Communications**
┈┈> USA

0955 ┈┈> **bonbon london**
┈┈> UK

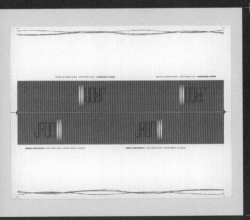

0956 ┈┈> **Hollis Brand Communications**
┈┈> USA

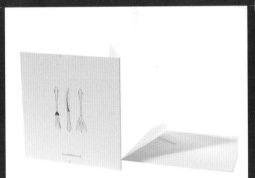

0957 ┈┈> **The Design Laboratory**
┈┈> UK

0958 ⋯▸ S&N Design
⋯▸ USA

0959 ⇢ Fullblastinc.com
⇢ USA

0960 ⇢ Braue Strategic Brand Design
⇢ Germany

0961 ⇢ Fullblastinc.com
⇢ USA

0962 ⇢ David Caunce
⇢ UK

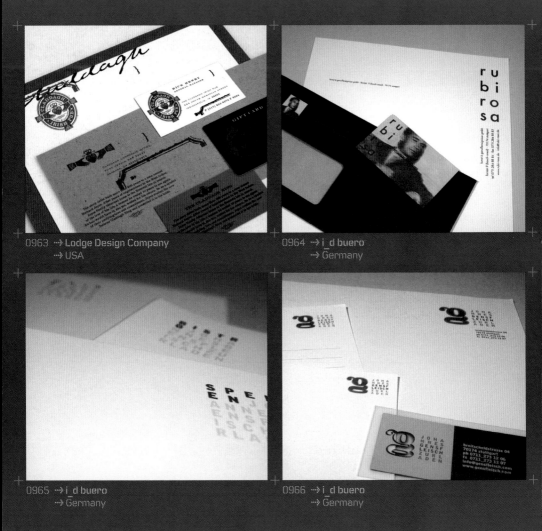

0963 ⋯→ **Lodge Design Company**
⋯→ USA

0964 ⋯→ **i_d buero**
⋯→ Germany

0965 ⋯→ **i_d buero**
⋯→ Germany

0966 ⋯→ **i_d buero**
⋯→ Germany

0968 ···⟶ Willoughby Design Group
   ···⟶ USA

0969 ···⟶ Bakken Creative Company
   ···⟶ USA

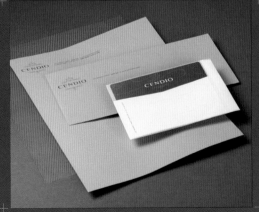

0970 ···⟶ Hollis Brand Communications
   ···⟶ USA

0971 ···⟶ Inaria
   ···⟶ UK

0973 ⇢ Bakken Creative Company
⇢ USA

0974 ⇥ Octavo Design Pty Ltd
⇥ Australia

0975 ⇥ Octavo Design Pty Ltd
⇥ Australia

0976 ⇥ Octavo Design Pty Ltd
⇥ Australia

0977 ⇥ Poulin & Morris
⇥ USA

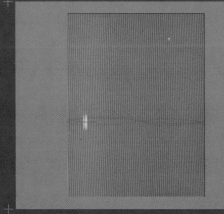

0978 ⋯› **Hollis Brand Communications**
⋯› USA

0979 ⋯› **Bakken Creative Company**
⋯› USA

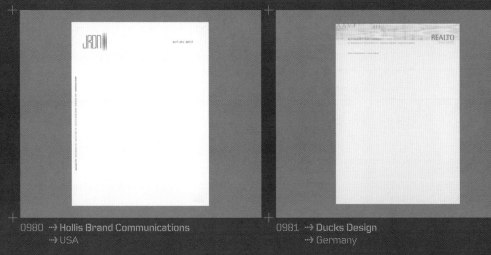

0980 ⋯› **Hollis Brand Communications**
⋯› USA

0981 ⋯› **Ducks Design**
⋯› Germany

bezu

FRENCH·ASIAN CUISINE

0982 ⋯→ From Scratch Design Studio
     ⋯→ USA

0983 ⟶ Mirko Ilić Corp.
⟶ USA

0984 ⤳ On The Edge Design, Inc
⤳ USA

0985 ⤳ On The Edge Design, Inc
⤳ USA

0986 ⤳ On The Edge Design, Inc
⤳ USA

0987 ⤳ On The Edge Design, Inc
⤳ USA

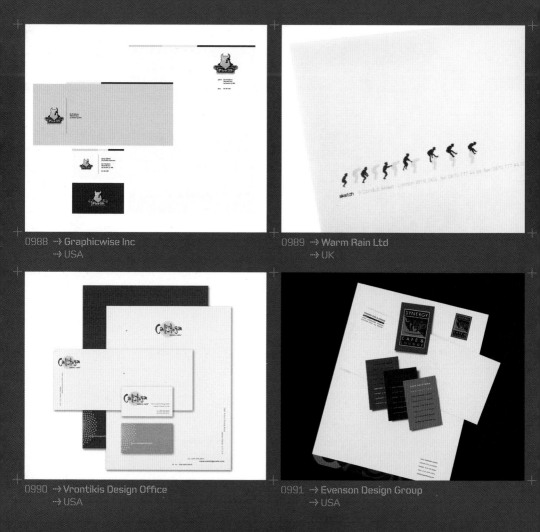

0988 ⟶ Graphicwise Inc
⟶ USA

0989 ⟶ Warm Rain Ltd
⟶ UK

0990 ⟶ Vrontikis Design Office
⟶ USA

0991 ⟶ Evenson Design Group
⟶ USA

0992 ⋯▶ Regan Blough
　　 ⋯▶ USA

0993 ⋯▶ biz-R
　　 ⋯▶ UK

0994 ⋯▶ AdamsMorioka
　　 ⋯▶ USA

0995 ⋯▶ Betty Soldi
　　 ⋯▶ UK

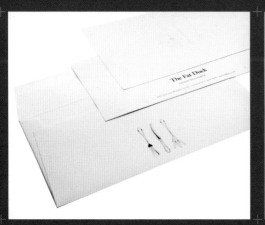

0996 ⇢ The Design Laboratory
⇢ UK

0997 ⇢ The Design Laboratory
⇢ UK

0998 ⇢ Crush Design & Art Direction
⇢ UK

0999 ⇢ Mary Hutchinson Design LLC
⇢ USA

CAFÉ

fina flor

ALFREDO HIDALGO
ANDREA RATTON

R. Estrada do Mucugê, 69-B
Arraial D'Ajuda BA
Cep 45810-000
cafefinaflor@hotmail.com

CHAPTER 7
END MATTER

28 Limited Brand
Bessemerstrasse 85, Halle 8
44793 Bochum
Germany
+49 234 91 609 51
www.twenty-eight.de

0185, 0186, 0187, 0188
Art Director: Mirco Kurth
Designer: Mirco Kurth
Client: Maluma

804© Graphic Design
Ronsdorfer Strasse 77a
40233 Düsseldorf
Germany
+49 (0) 211 77 92 760
www.achtnullvier.de

0420, 0474, 0475, 0476, 0477,
0735, 0770, 0901
Art Directors: Helge Dirk Rieder,
Oliver Henn
Designers: Helge Dirk Rieder,
Oliver Henn
Client: Mielert's

A10 Design
Rua Helena, 170
4º Andar
Vila Olimpia São Paulo SP
Brazil
+55 (11) 38453503
www.a10.com.br

0063, 0064, 0079, 0516, 0517
Art Director: Margarete Takeda
Designer: Maria Costa Lino
Client: A Bela Sintra

AdamsMorioka
8484 Wilshire Blvd., Suite 600
Beverly Hills, CA 90211
USA
323-966-5990
www.adamsmorioka.com

0098, 0099, 0218, 0532, 0910
Art Director: Noreen Morioka
Designer: Noreen Morioka
Client: Nic's

0124, 0994
Art Directors: Sean Adams,
Noreen Morioka
Designers: Sean Adams,
Noreen Morioka
Client: Theater Square Grill

0125, 0342, 0479, 0749
Art Directors: Sean Adams,
Noreen Morioka
Designers: Sean Adams,
Noreen Morioka
Client: Fusion at PDC

0291, 0657, 0750
Art Directors: Sean Adams,
Noreen Morioka
Designers: Sean Adams,
Noreen Morioka
Client: Encounter

Adrienne Weiss Corporation
c/o The Levy Restaurants
980 N Michigan Ave. Suite 400
Chicago, IL 60611
USA

0603
Client: DIVE! Los Angeles and DIVE!
Las Vegas (The Levy Restaurants/
Steven Spielberg and Jeffrey
Katzenberger)

Advance Design Centre
2501 Oak Lawn Ave., Suite 200
Dallas, TX 75219
USA
214-526-1420
www.adc-inc.com

0209
Art Director: Doug Livingston
Designer: Doug Livingston
Client: Georgie's Chow House

0210
Art Director: Doug Livingston
Designer: Christine Pasienski
Client: Ravelo's Pastaria

0213
Art Director: Doug Livingston
Designer: Jesus Acosta
Client: Pollo Campero

0240
Art Director: Doug Livingston
Designer: Christine Pasienski
Client: Milano's

Adventure Advertising
PO Box 576
Camden, ME 04843
USA

0647
Art Director/ Designer: Joseph
Ryan
Illustrator: Jerry Sterman
Client: Sea Dog Brewing Company

Alexander Design Associates
8 West 19th St.
Suite 2A
New York, NY 10011
USA
212-807-6641

0162
Art Director: Dean Alexander
Designer: Kelly Tamaki
Client: Restaurant Associates
(Tropica Caribbean Seafood)

Allies
108 Great Portland St.
London W1W 6PG
UK
+44 0 20 7636 3377
www.alliesdesign.com

0502, 0503, 0504
Art Director: Susanna Cook
Designer: Colin Smith
Client: Kyle Cathie Publishers Ltd

0505, 0506
Art Director: Susanna Cook
Designer: Amy Joyce
Client: B@1

Annabelle Wimer Design
539 Polk Blvd.
Suite B
Des Moines, IA 50312
USA
515-255-4953

0627
Art Director: Annabel Wimer
Designer: Annabel Wimer
Client: Steve Villmain (The Diner)

Art Institute of California, Orange County
3601 West Sunflower Ave.
Santa Ana, CA 92704
Mailing address: 10 Thunder Run
6-d
Irvine, CA 92614
USA
949-551-5662
www.artinstitutes.edu/
orangecounty
atiragram3@hotmail.com

0224
Art Director: Maggie Vazquez, MFA
Designer: J-R Ignacio
Client: A-Sushi

0249
Art Director: Maggie Vazquez, MFA
Designer: Simson Chanta
Client: Tres Hermanos

Artie Horowitz Design
632 South Highland Ave.
Los Angeles, CA 90036
USA

0682
Art Director:
Designer: Artie Horowitz
Client: Maria's Cucina (Boris
Brezinger)

Associates Design
3177 MacArthur Blvd.
Northbrook, IL 60062
USA

0519
Art Director: Chuck Polonsky
Designer: Beth Finn
Client: Banners, FleetCenter
Boston (Sportservice)

0558
Art Director: Chuck Polonsky
Designer: Shirley Bonk
Client: Marriott Philadelphia
Airport

0559
Art Director: Chuck Polonsky
Designer: Bobbie Serafini
Client: Allie's American Grille
(Marriott Hotels)

0599
Art Director: Chuck Polonsky
Designer: Jill Arena
Client: Oceana (Marriott Hotels)

0624, 0625, 0626
Art Director: Chuck Polonsky
Designer: Jill Arena
Computer Artist: John Arena
Client: All Seasons Café (Hyatt
Hotels Corp.)

0630
Art Director: Chuck Polonsky
Designer: Beth Finn
Client: Grand Hyatt (Humu Humu)

0631
Art Director: Chuck Polonsky
Designer: Jill Arena
Client: Sportservice

0645
Art Director: Chuck Polonsky
Designer: Mary Greco
Client: Legends, FleetCenter
Boston (Sportservice)

0651, 0664
Art Director: Chuck Polonsky
Designer: Jill Arena
Client: Prairie Knights Casino
(Seven Circles)

0660
Art Director: Chuck Polonsky
Designer: Roberta Serafini
Client: Hyatt Orlando Airport
(Hemisphere)

Ayse Çelem
Birinci Cadde No. 89
Arnavutköy
Istanbul 34345
Turkey
+90 0212 358 20 93
www.aysecelemdesign.com

0412, 0413, 0414, 0950
Art Director: Ayse Çelem
Designer: Ayse Çelem
Client: Ulus 29 Restaurant

Bakken Creative Company
1250 Addison, Studio 208
Berkeley, CA 94702
USA
510-540-8260
www.bakkencreativeco.co

0447, 0769, 0915
Art Director: Michelle Bakken
Designer: Jennifer Chan
Client: Firefly, Kimpton Group

0472
Art Director: Michelle Bakken
Designer: Gina Mondello
Client: South Water Kitchen,
Kimpton Group

0916, 0973, 0979
Art Director: Michelle Bakken
Designer: Gina Mondello
Client: Three Degrees, Larkspur
Hospitality

0969
Art Director: Michelle Bakken
Designer: Gina Mondello
Client: Bar Rouge, Kimpton Group

Bartosz Oczujda
ul. Włodkowica 3/5
Poznań Wielkopolska 60-334
Poland
+48 505 180 482
b9999@o2.pl

0850
Art Director: Bartosz Oczujda
Designer: Bartosz Oczujda
Client: Pożegnanie z Afryką

BASELINE
Office 71, Stirling Business Centre
Stirling
FK8 2DZ Scotland
UK
01786 430 378
www.selinegraphics.co.uk

0357, 0473
Art Director: Doulas Walker
Designer: Steven Bonner
Client: Maclay Inns

0859
Art Director: Doulas Walker
Designer: Steven Bonner
Client: Conran Restaurants

Betty Soldi
29 Sheen Common Dr.
Richmond, Surrey
TW10 5BW
UK

0995
Art Director: Betty Soldi
Client: Arts Theatre Café (Phil
Owens, Jo Phillips)

BigEyes Design
31 Rothschild Blvd., Room 35
Tel Aviv 66883
Israel
+972 54 530 7229
lehav@bigeyes.co.il
bigeyes.express@gmail.com

**0096, 0097, 0192, 0211, 0251,
0492, 0493, 0494, 0495, 0496,
0497, 0498, 0499, 0500, 0501,
0533, 0537, 0538, 0539, 0540,
0541, 0696, 0697, 0707, 0804,
0805**
Art Director: Lahav Halevy
Designer: Lahav Halevy
Client: R2M Corporation

biz-R
35A Fore St.
Totnes, Devon TQ95HN
UK
+44 01803 868989
www.biz-r.co.uk
retail@biz-r.co.uk

**0422, 0423, 0681, 0726, 0788,
0993**
Art Director: Blair Thomson
Designer: Tish England
Client: Effings

bonbon london
F5, 13 The Paragon
London
UK
+44 07932 008 225
www.bonbonlondon.com
studio@bonbonlondon.com

**0100, 0254, 0701, 0796, 0814,
0815, 0927, 0928, 0951, 0952,
0953**
Art Directors: Mark Harper,
Sasha Castling
Designer: Mark Harper
Client: Jill Bartlett & Company

**0101, 0136, 0255, 0418, 0520,
0583, 0734, 0774, 0834, 0922**
Art Directors: Mark Harper,
Sasha Castling
Designer: Mark Harper
Client: Cafeteria 124

**0372, 0419, 0448, 0450, 0451,
0522, 0686, 0687, 0688, 0689,
0717, 0795, 0821, 0822, 0863,
0877, 0878, 0905, 0937, 0939**
Art Directors: Mark Harper,
Sasha Castling
Designer: Mark Harper
Client: Smiths of Smithfield

Bowhaus Design Groupe
340 North 12th St., Suite 314
Philadelphia, PA 19107
USA
215-733-0603
www.bowhausdesign.com
info@bowhausdesign.com

0238, 0949
Art Director: Matt O'Rourke
Designer: Matt Labul
Client: MilkBoy Coffee

0276
Art Director: Matt O'Rourke
Designer: Matt O'Rourke
Client: Fiso

Brandhouse WTS
10A Frederick Close
London W2 2HD
UK
+44 020 7262 1707
www.brandhouse.co.uk/flash.html
kj@brandhousewts.com

0061, 0110, 0243, 0491
Art Director: Dave Beard
Designer: Bronwen Edwards
Client: Mitchells and Butlers

**0081, 0082, 0490, 0511, 0772,
0806, 0808, 0810**
Art Director: Dave Beard
Designer: Bronwen Edwards
Client: 43 South Molton Street

0219, 0509
Art Director: Dave Beard
Designer: Keely Jackman
Client: Mitchells and Butlers

0510
Art Director: Dave Beard
Designer: Mel Maynard
Client: Mitchells and Butlers

0529
Art Director: Dave Beard
Designer: Emma Staveacre
Client: Mitchells and Butlers

Braue Strategic Brand Design
Eiswerkestrasse 8
27572 Bremerhaven
Germany
+49 0471 983 82 0
www.braue.info

0138, 0268, 0515, 0831, 0960
Art Director: Marçel Robbers
Designer: Marçel Robbers
Client: Restaurant Leuchtfeuer

0391, 0514, 0782
Art Director: Kai Braue
Designers: Marçel Robbers,
Sandra Blum
Client: Caffè Bene

Bright & Associates
901 Abbotkinney
Venice, CA 90291
USA

0663, 0725
Art Directors: Bill Corridori,
Keith Bright
Designer: Bill Corridori
Client: Gratis Restaurant

Bullet Communications Inc
200 South Midland Ave.
Joliet, IL 60435
USA

0297, 0658
Designer: Tim Scott
Client: Pizza Picasso

0685
Designer: Tim Scott
Client: Stella D'Italia Restaurant

Campus Collection
PO Box 2904
Tuscaloosa, AL 35403
USA
205-758-0678
www.campuscollection.net

0201, 0888
Art Director: Joe Rossomanno
Designer: Phillip Sanford
Client: Starlite Diner

0337
Art Director: Joe Rossomano
Designer: Courtney Dagenhart
Client: Keys Fisheries

0338
Art Director: Joe Rossomano
Designer: Tony Brock
Client: Sam's Corner

0390
Designer: Tony Brock
Client: Rosie's Tamale House

0883
Art Director: Joe Rossomano
Designer: Debbie Lewis
Client: Cuban Rooster

0884
Art Director: Joe Rossomano
Designer: Larry McAfee
Client: Bumpers

0885
Art Director: Joe Rossomano
Designer: Lulu Kaufman
Client: Blue Heaven

0887
Art Director: Joe Rossomano
Designer: Pam Bullington
Client: Pat O'Brien's

0889
Art Director: Joe Rossomano
Client: Mad Hatter's

0890
Art Director: Joe Rossomano
Designer: Debbie Lewis
Client: Conch Republic

0891
Art Director: Joe Rossomano
Designers: Pam Bullington,
Neal Cross
Client: Hello Deli

0892
Art Director: Joe Rossomano
Designer: Pam Bullington
Client: Frostbites

CDI Studios
2215-A Renaissance Dr.
Las Vegas, NV 89119
USA
702-876-3316
www.cdistudios.com

0236, 0897
Art Director: Dan McElhattan III
Illustrator: David Araujo
Client: Bleu Gourmet

0281
Art Director: Dan McElhattan III
Designer: Dan McElhattan III
Client: Osaka Sushi Bar

0293, 0876
Art Director: Dan McElhattan III
Designers: Dan McElhattan III,
David Araujo
Client: Gasoline Alley

0316
Art Director: Dan McElhattan III
Designer: Dan McElhattan III
Client: Northside Nathan's

0324, 0674
Art Director: Victoria Hart
Designer: Brian Felgar
Client: Julie Anne's Bakery, Café &
Fine Foods

0329
Art Director: Dan McElhattan III
Designers: Dan McElhattan III,
Alfred Herczeg

Chris Rooney
1317 Santa Fe Ave.
Berkeley, CA 94702
USA
415-827-3729
looneyrooney@mindspring.com

0764
Designer: Chris Rooney
Client: Tastings

christiansen: creative
511 2nd St., Suite 203
Hudson, WI 54016
USA
715-381-8480
www.christiansencreative.com

**0062, 0105, 0468, 0469, 0557,
0902**
Art Directors: Dave MacDonald,
Tricia Christiansen
Designers: Dave MacDonald,
Tricia Christiansen
Client: Bricks Neapolitan Pizza

Coco Raynes Graphics, Inc.
35 Newbury St.
Boston, MA 02116
USA
617-536-9052

0685
Art Director: Coco Raynes
Designers: Coco Raynes,
Brian Erickson
Client: Lou Lou's Rotisserie

Commarts Inc
1112 Pearl St.
Boulder, CO 80302
USA
303-447-8202
www.commartsdesign.com

0193, 0349
Art Director: Mark Jasin
Designer: Mark Jasin
Client: Cortex Companies

0294
Art Director: Richard Foy
Designer: Jeff Keil
Client: Laudisio's Restaurant

Corbin Design
109 East Front St. #304
Traverse City, MI 49684
USA
616-947-1236

0637
Art Director: Jeffry Corbin
Designer: Janet Mortensen
Client: Joe Bologna (Rookies
Clubhouse)

Crush Design & Art Direction
6 Gloucester St.
Brighton BN1 4EW
UK
+44 0 1273 60 60 58
www.crushed.co.uk
contact@crushed.co.uk

0094, 0427, 0802, 0823, 0998
Art Director: Carl Rush
Designers: Tim Diacon,
Chris Pelling, Simon Slater
Client: Scoundrels Ltd

0247, 0425, 0426
Art Director: Carl Rush
Designer: Simon Slater
Client: Medicine Bar

CWA Inc.
4015 Ibis St.
San Diego, CA 92103
USA
619-299-0431

0748
Art Director: Susan Merritt
Designer: Christy Van Deman
Illustrator: Susan Merritt
Client: Koll International (La Paloma
at Palmilla)

Damion Hickman Design
1760 Kaiser Ave.
Irvine, CA 92614
USA
949-261-7857
www.damionhickman.com

0031, 0137
Art Director: Damion Hickman
Designer: Leighton Hubbell
Client: Ten Restaurant

0333
Art Director: Damion Hickman
Designer: Colin Freeman
Client: Sutra Lounge

0335
Art Director: Damion Hickman
Designer: Leighton Hubbell
Client: Ten Restaurant

0336
Art Director: Damion Hickman
Designer: Leighton Hubbell
Client: Tentation

0356
Art Director: Damion Hickman
Designer: Billi Rakov
Client: Blush Lounge

David Carter Design
4112 Swiss Ave.
Dallas, TX 75204
USA

0576, 0577
Art Director: Lori Wilson
Designers: Lori Wilson,
Gary Lobue, Jr.
Client: Spike's Jazz Bar (Hotel
Principe Felipe)

0642
Designer: Sharon LeJeune
Client: Anzu

David Caunce
67 Acres Rd.
Chorlton
Manchester M21 9EB
UK
+44 0161 861 9309
www.imagine-cga.co.uk

0327, 0344, 0453, 0454, 0455,
0456, 0457, 0675, 0676, 0677,
0702, 0703, 0827, 0872, 0962
Art Director: David Caunce
Designer: David Caunce
Client: The Bean Counter

Dean Johnson Design
646 Massachusetts Ave.
Indianapolis, IN 46250
USA
317-634-8020
www.deanjohnson.com

0303
Art Director: Mike Schwab
Designers: Mike Schwab,
Bruce Dean
Client: Mo'Joe Coffeehouse

0317
Art Director: Mike Schwab
Designer: Mike Schwab
Client: Loughmiller's Pub & Eatery

0614
Art Director:
Designers: Mike Schwab,
Bruce Dean
Client: Some Guys Pizza

The Design Laboratory
The Design Laboratory at the
Innovation Center
Central Saint Martins College of
Art and Design
Southampton Row
London WC1B 4AP
UK
+44 0 20 7514 7028
www.designlaboratory.co.uk

0404, 0405, 0406, 0407, 0408,
0670, 0907, 0908, 0957, 0996,
0997
Art Directors: Brent Richards,
Yann Mathias
Designers: Milos Covic,
Eva Helberger
Client: The Fat Duck Restaurant

Disney Design Group
Walt Disney World
PO Box 10,000
Lake Buena Vista, FL 32830-1000
USA

0556
Art Directors: Jeff Morris,
Renee Schneider
Designer: Mimi Palladino
Illustrator: Michael Mohjer
Writer: Tony Fernandez
Client: Bonfamille's Cafe (Disney
Port Orleans Resort)

0597, 0609
Art Directors: Jeff Morris,
Renee Schneider
Designers: Thomas Scott,
Michael Mohjer
Illustrator: Michael Mohjer
Client: Crockett's Tavern (Disney's
Fort Wilderness Resort)

0608
Art Directors: Jeff Morris,
Renee Schneider
Designer: Mimi Palladino
Illustrator: Michael Mohjer
Writer: Tony Fernandez
Client: Whispering Canyon Café
(Disney's Wilderness Lodge)

0617
Art Directors: Jeff Morris,
Renee Schneider
Designer: Mimi Palladino
Illustrator: Peter Emslie
Client: Narcoosee's (Disney's Grand
Floridian Beach Resort)

Dornig Graphic Design
Saegerstrasse 4
A-6850 Dornbirn
Austria
0043 664 1438374
dornig@saegenvier.at

0221, 0222, 0785, 0862
Art Director: Kurt Dornig
Designer: Kurt Dornig
Client: Theater Café

Ducks Design
Goetheallee 19
22765 Hamburg
Germany
+49 40 38083889
www.ducksdesign.de
contact@ducksdesign.de

0265, 0379
Art Director: Ray Nher
Designer: Ray Nher
Client: Events Promotion EPA

0271
Art Director: Ray Nher
Designer: Ray Nher
Client: Titanic

0332, 0741, 0871, 0981.
Art Director: Kay Penndorf
Designer: Kay Penndorf
Client: Realto

0355, 0542, 0543, 0545, 0807
Art Director: Ray Nher
Designer: Ray Nher
Client: Trips'e Bock

The Dunlavey Studio
3576 McKinley Blvd.
Suite 200
Sacramento, CA 95816
USA
916-451-2170

0067
Art Director: Michael Dunlavey
Designer: Michael Dunlavey
Client: Java City at Market Square

01.23, 01.53, 01.54, 01.55
Art Director: Michael Dunlavey
Designer: Michael Dunlavey
Client: Jeff Tay (Fabulous 50's
Café)

DZ6 Design
Av. Nova York, No. 294, Casa 1
Porto Alegre RS 90550-070
Brazil
+55 51 3342 2725
www.dz6.com.br
dz6@dz6.com.br

0659, 091.4
Art Director: Janine Moura
Client: Constantino Café

Eilts Anderson Tracy
4111 Baltimore
Kansas City, MO 64111
USA
816-931-2687

0653
Art Director: Patrice Eilts
Designer: Patrice Eilts
Illustrator: Patrice Eilts
Client: PB&J Restaurants (Coyote
Grill)

Elephant Design Pvt Ltd
13, Kumar Srushti
Bavdhan
Pune, Maharashtra, 411. 021.
India
+91. 20 22951.059
www.elephantdesign.com

0040, 01.03, 0398
Art Directors: Ashwini Deshpande,
Ashish Deshpande
Designer: Sheetal, Nitin
Client: Hindustan Lever Limited

Elfen
20 Harrowby Lane
Cardiff Bay
Cardiff CF10 5GN
Wales
+44 0 29 2048 4824
www.elfen.co.uk
post@elfen.co.uk

0070, 0835
Art Director: Guto Evans
Designer: Matthew James
Client: Armless Dragon

0075, 01.49
Art Director: Guto Evans
Designer: Wayne Harris
Client: Café Junior

Emma Main
PO Box 11.-331. Wellington
Harcourts Building, Suite 316
22 Grey St.
New Zealand

0666
Art Director: Emma Main
Photographer: Kerry MacKay
Typesetter: Alistair Best
Sinage Sculptures: Andrew
"Floppy" Beattie, Peter Hutchinson
Client: Mondo Cucina, Wellington,
New Zealand

Etc Diseño Gráfico
CC Las Tapias, Nivel 2 Local
14 Mérida
Mailing address: Urb La Mara
Calle 5 Qta. Ta'lluvia
Mérida
Venezuela 51.01
Venezuela
biancaprado@gmail.com

01.80
Art Director: Bianca Prado
Designers: Bianca Prado,
Luisa Prado
Client: Food Planet

0252
Art Director: Bianca Prado
Designers: Bianca Prado,
Luisa Prado
Client: Rudy's Pizza

Evenson Design Group
4445 Overland Ave.
Culver City, CA 90230
USA
310-204-1995
www.evensondesign.com
edgmail@evensondesign.com

0171
Art Director: Stan Evenson
Designer: John Lovause
Client: Cubby's Coffeehouse

0174
Art Director: Stan Evenson
Designer: Katja Loesch
Client: Synergy

0396, 0714, 0875
Art Directors: Stan Evenson,
Mark Sojka
Designer: John Lovause
Client: Cubby's Coffeehouse

0397
Art Directors: Stan Evenson,
Mark Sojka
Designer: Katja Loesch
Client: Synergy

0991
Art Directors: Stan Evenson,
Mark Sojka
Designer: Katja Loesch
Client: Synergy

Eye Speak
235 S Main St., Suite A
Jonesboro, AR 72401
USA
870-530-2541
www.eyespeakvc.com

0288
Art Director: Kimberly Boyd
Vickrey
Designer: Kimberly Boyd Vickrey
Client: Club Luna

0299
Art Director: Kimberly Boyd
Vickrey
Designer: Kimberly Boyd Vickrey
Client: Pieros

0302
Art Directors: Kimberly Boyd
Vickrey, Eric Vickrey
Designer: Lisa Carter
Client: Envisions Smelly Cat Shak

Fabrice Praeger
54 bis, rue de l'Érmitage
75020 Paris
France
01 60 33 17 00
fabrice.praeger@wanadoo.fr

0417, 0623, 0900, 0912, 0946,
0947, 0948
Art Director: Fabrice Praeger
Designer: Fabrice Praeger
Client: Tahiti/ Reflet/ La Petite
Épicerie

Finest/Magma
Südenstr. 52
76135 Karlsruhe
Germany
+49 721 831.422 0
www.finestmagma.com
info@finestmagma.com

0065, 0095, 0259, 0261, 0430,
0773, 0789, 0790, 0791
Art Director: Lars Harmsen
Designer: Lars Harmsen
Client: Café Bar 53

0273, 0274, 0277, 0535, 0751,
0752
Art Director: Lars Harmsen
Designers: Sandra Augstein,
Ulrich Weiß
Client: G. Braun Verlag

Fitch
1266 Manning Parkway
Powell, OH 43065
USA
614-885-3453
www.fitch.com

0051, 0052, 0059
Art Director: Brian Harvey
Designer: Bill Weikart
Client: Taberna del Tequila, Sky
Harbor

0053, 0054, 0060
Art Director: Brian Harvey
Designer: Bill Weikart
Client: Expedia.com Café

0055, 0066
Art Director: David Denniston
Designer: Paul Teeples
Client: Caribou Coffee

0057, 0058
Art Director: Brian Harvey
Designer: Bill Weikart
Client: Pei Wei Asian Diner

0073
Art Director: Brian Harvey
Designer: Bill Weikart
Client: Chef Jimmy's

Fresh Oil
251 Cottage St.
Pawtucket, RI 02860
USA
401-709-4656
www.freshoil.com

0263
Art Director: Dan Stebbings
Designer: Dan Stebbings
Client: 22 Bowen's

0306
Art Director: Dan Stebbings
Designer: Dan Stebbings
Client: Ollie's Noodle Shop & Grille

0307, 0813
Art Director: Dan Stebbings
Designers: Dan Stebbings,
Nelson Couto
Client: pb's Diner

0308
Art Director: Dan Stebbings
Designer: Dan Stebbings
Client: Cowesett Inn

0312
Art Director: Dan Stebbings
Designers: Dan Stebbings,
Nelson Couto
Client: Sonoma - California Café

0315, 0534, 0826
Art Director: Dan Stebbings
Designer: Nelson Couto
Client: Red Stripe - An American
Brasserie

0345
Art Director: Dan Stebbings
Designer: Dan Stebbings
Client: XO Steakhouse

0346
Art Director: Dan Stebbings
Designer: Nelson Couto
Client: China Sky

0358, 0359
Art Director: Dan Stebbings
Designers: Dan Stebbings,
Nelson Couto
Client: Madhouse Café

0373, 0375
Art Director: Dan Stebbings
Designer: Dan Stebbings
Client: Siena-Tuscan Soul Food

0376
Art Director: Dan Stebbings
Designer: Dan Stebbings
Client: Toù Bagaille

0536
Art Director: Dan Stebbings
Designer: Dan Stebbings
Client: Café Newport

From Scratch Design Studio
1325 G St. NW, Suite 500
Washington, DC 20005
USA
202-449-7652
www.fromscratch.us

0220, 0489, 0944, 0945, 0982
Art Director: Cristian Strittmatter
Designer: Cristian Strittmatter
Client: Bezu (Eddie Benaim)

0269, 0471, 0738
Art Director: Cristian Strittmatter
Designer: Cristian Strittmatter
Client: Rasika (Knightsbridge
Management)

Frost Design, Sydney
Level 1, 15 Foster St.
Surry Hills, NSW 2010
Australia
+61 2 9280 4233
www.frostdesign.com.au

0049, 0050
Art Director: Vince Frost
Client: Sydney Dance Cafe

**0147, 0866, 0867, 0868, 0919,
0920**
Art Director: Vince Frost
Client: Nautilus Group (Coast
Restaurant)

**0523, 0524, 0525, 0526, 0812,
0918**
Art Director: Vince Frost
Client: Nautilus Group (Manta
Restaurant)

Fullblastinc.com
618 NW Glisan, #200
Portland, OR 97209
USA
503-227-2002
www.fullblastinc.com
design@fullblastinc.com

**0152, 0554, 0830, 0886, 0959,
0961**
Art Director: N. Todd Skiles
Designer: N. Todd Skiles
Client: Park Kitchen

0242
Art Director: N. Todd Skiles
Designer: N. Todd Skiles
Client: Max's Fanno Creek Brew
Pub

0527
Art Director: N. Todd Skiles
Designer: N. Todd Skiles
Client: Blueplate

0528, 0531
Art Director: N. Todd Skiles
Designer: N. Todd Skiles
Client: Vita Café

**Gabriel Kalach - Visual
Communication**
1000 West Ave., #1004
Miami Beach, FL 33139
USA
305-532-2336
proartgraphics@mac.com

0253
Art Director: Gabriel Kalach
Designer: Gabriel Kalach
Client: Arrso Restaurants

0256
Art Director: Gabriel Kalach
Designer: Gabriel Kalach
Client: 820 Gotham Bar

0262
Art Director: Gabriel Kalach
Designer: Gabriel Kalach
Client: 62 Bar Lounge

0311
Art Director: Gabriel Kalach
Designer: Gabriel Kalach
Client: Mas Allá Restaurant

0318
Art Director: Gabriel Kalach
Designer: Gabriel Kalach
Client: 820 Bar – Restaurant

0381, 0382
Art Director: Gabriel Kalach
Designer: Gabriel Kalach
Client: Karu&Y

0384
Art Director: Gabriel Kalach
Designer: Gabriel Kalach
Client: Mas Allá Restaurant

0385
Art Director: Gabriel Kalach
Designer: Gabriel Kalach
Client: Capisce? Restaurant

0394
Art Director: Gabriel Kalach
Designer: Gabriel Kalach
Client: Gaira Café

Gingerbee Creative
44 N. Last Chance Gulch
Helena, MT 59601
USA
406-443-3032
www.gingerbee.com

0242
Designer: Ginger Knaff
Client: Moose Magoo's

Gloria Paul
150 W. Jefferson Ave.
Suite 100
Detroit, MI 48226
USA

0629, 0632
Art Director: Gloria Paul
Client: Cup·A·Cino Coffee House
(Jennifer Bell)

Graphic Content
600 N Bishop Ave., Suite 200
Dallas, TX 75208
USA
214-948-6969
www.graphiccontent.com

0480
Art Director: Art Garcia
Designer: Art Garcia
Client: Marie Gabrile

0481
Art Directors: Art Garcia,
Jesus Nava
Designer: Josh Weatherspoon
Client: Campuzano Restaurant

0731
Art Director: Art Garcia
Client: Marie Gabrile

Graphicwise Inc
PO Box 53801
Irvine, CA 92619
USA
949-859-0767
www.graphicwise.com
info@graphicwise.com

01.98, 0587, 0988
Art Director: Kevin Javid
Designer: Art Javid
Client: Pier39

Greiner Design Associates
311.1 N. Ravenswood
Chicago, IL 60657
USA
312-404-0210

0043, 0045
Art Director: John Greiner
Photographer: Hedrich/Blessing
Client: Art Institute of Chicago
(Court Cafeteria)

Greteman Group
142 North Mosley
Wichita, KS 67202
USA

01.67
Art Director: Sonia Greteman
Designers: Sonia Greteman,
Jo Quillin, Chris Parks
Client: Oaxaca Grill

Hamagami/Carroll, Inc
1316 3rd Street Promenade,
Suite 305
Santa Monica, CA 90401
USA
310-458-7600

0115, 0116, 0117, 0118, 0119
Client: Disney

Hand Made Group
Via Sartori, 18
52017 Stia (AR)
Italy
+39 0575 582083
www.hmg.it

0264, 0572, 0573, 081.8
Art Director: Alessandro Esteri
Designer: Davide Premuni
Client: La Tartine

Hans Flink Design Inc.
11 Martine Ave.
White Plains, NY 10606
USA
914-328-0888

0722, 0723
Art Director: Hans D. Flink and
staff
Client: Grand Central Oyster Bar &
Restaurant

Hansen Associates
2900-100 Fourth Ave.
San Diego, CA 92103-5987
USA
619-233-0422
www.hansenassociates.net

0212
Art Director: Ted Hansen
Designer: Colleen Carr
Client: Oasis Bar & Grill

Hardy Design
Rua Araguari 1.541
5º Andar 301.90-111
Belo Horizonte
Brazil
+55 31 3275 3095
www.hardydesign.com.br

0521, 0585, 0923, 1.000
Art Director: Mariana Hardy
Designers: Andréa Gomes,
Carolina Marini, Mariana Hardy
Client: Café Fina Flor

Hat-Trick Design
3 Morollo St, Third Floor
London SE1 3HB
UK
+44 0 20 74037875
www.hat-trickdesign.co.uk

0046, 0047
Art Directors: David Kimpton,
Jim Sutherland, Gareth Howat
Designer: Ben Christie
Client: The Salvation Army

0048
Art Directors: David Kimpton,
Jim Sutherland, Gareth Howat
Designer: Alex Swatridge
Client: Xchanging

Heather Heflin
CAA Box 801
Bloomfield Hills, MI 48303
USA

0574, 0575
Art Director: Heather Heflin
Client: Farah's on the Avenue
(Nick Farah)

Heinzle Design
1060 Vienna
Austria
+43 1 5860852
www.heinzledesign.at
office@heinzledesign.at

0272, 0546, 0562
Art Director: Lothar Aemilian
Heinzle
Designer: Markus Maier
Client: Reflex

Hollis Brand Communications
680 West Beech St., Suite 1
San Diego, CA 92101
USA
619-234-2061
www.hollisbc.com

0020, 0141, 0513, 0646, 0777,
0942, 0943, 0954, 0956, 0978,
0980
Art Director: Don Hollis
Designers: Don Hollis,
Angela Villareal
Client: Jordan Restaurant

0080, 0150, 0156, 0512, 0588,
0589, 0778, 0792, 0809, 0940,
0941
Art Director: Don Hollis
Designer: Don Hollis
Client: Chive

0120, 0548, 0793, 0828
Art Director: Don Hollis
Designer: Don Hollis
Client: D-lush Deluxe Beverage
Joint

0787
Art Director: Don Hollis
Designers: Don Hollis,
Angela Villareal
Client: Blanca Restaurant

0803, 0970
Art Director: Don Hollis
Designer: Don Hollis
Client: Cendio

Hornall Anderson Design Works
710 2nd Ave., Suite 1300
Seattle, WA 98104
USA
206-826-2329
www.hadw.com

0032, 0033, 0034, 0035, 0036,
0038, 0144, 0148, 0672, 0700,
0704, 0711, 0712, 0713, 0854
Art Director: Jack Anderson
Designers: James Tee, Sonja Max
Client: Terra Vida Coffee

0037, 0551
Art Directors: Lisa Cerveny,
James Tee, Tiffany Place
Client: Tahitian Noni

0719, 0836, 0853
Art Directors: Jack Anderson,
Larry Anderson
Designers: Larry Anderson,
Elmer de la Cruz, Bruce Stigler,
Jay Hilburn, Dorothee Soechting,
Don Stayner
Client: Widmer Brothers Brewery

0720, 0855, 0856
Art Directors: Jack Anderson,
Larry Anderson
Designers: Larry Anderson, Elmer
de la Cruz, Bruce Stigler, Jay
Hilburn, Bruce Branson-Meyer
Client: Widmer Brothers Brewery

0721, 0852
Art Directors: Jack Anderson,
Bruce Stigler
Designers: Larry Anderson,
Elmer de la Cruz, Bruce Stigler,
Jay Hilburn
Client: Widmer Brothers Brewery

Hunt Weber Clark Associates
525 Brannan St.
Suite 302
San Francisco, CA 94107
USA

0159
Art Director: Nancy Hunt-Weber
Designer: Nancy Hunt-Weber
Illustrator: Nancy Hunt-Weber
Client: Kimco Hotel and Restaurant
Management (Corona Bar & Grill)

0168
Art Director: Nancy Hunt-Weber
Designer: Gary Williams
Illustrators: Nancy Hunt-Weber,
Gary Williams
Client: Hawthorne Lane

i_d buero
Bismarkstrasse 67A
70197 Stuttgart
Germany
+49 (0) 711 636 8000
www.i-dbuero.de

**0004, 0005, 0087, 0113, 0352,
0402, 0403, 0745, 0898, 0899,
0909, 0964, 0965, 0966**
Art Director: Oliver A. Krimmel
Client: Rubirosa, Gensfleisch

Inaria
10 Plato Place
72-74 St Dionis Rd.
London SW6 4TU
UK
+44 0 20 7384 0904
www.inaria-design.com

0215, 0671, 0690, 0732, 0971
Art Directors: Andrew Thomas,
Debora Berardi
Designer: Anna Leaver
Client: Firezza

Jeff Fisher LogoMotives
PO Box 17155
Portland, OR 97217
USA
503-283-8673
www.fisherlogomotives.com

0203
Art Director: Jeff Fisher
Designer: Jeff Fisher
Client: North Bank Café

0207
Art Director: Jeff Fisher
Designer: Jeff Fisher
Client: Glo's Broiler

0208
Art Director: Jeff Fisher
Designer: Jeff Fisher
Client: Balaboosta Delicatessen

0380
Art Director: Jeff Fisher
Designer: Jeff Fisher
Client: La Patisserie

0598
Art Director: Todd Pierce
Designer: Jeff Fisher
Illustrator: Jeff Fisher
Client: Indies

John & Orna Designs
27 Belsize Lane
Belsize Mews Studio
London NW3 5AS
UK
+44 020 7431 9116
www.johnandornadesigns.co.uk
mail@johnandornadesigns.co.uk

0561, 0567, 0568
Art Director: John & Orna Designs
Designer: John & Orna Designs
Client: Stephen Lawrence
Charitable Trust

0569, 0570, 0571
Art Director: John & Orna Designs
Designer: John & Orna Designs
Client: Private client

John Evans Design
2200 North Lamar #220
Dallas, TX 75023
USA

0615
Art Director: Troy Scillian
Designer: John Evans
Illustrator: John Evans
Client: Pargo's (MBRK)

John Kneapler Design
48 West 21st St.
New York, NY 10010
USA
212-463-9774

0157
Art Director: John Kneapler
Designers: John Kneapler, Matt
Waldman, Daymon Bruck
Client: Stephan Loffredo, Thalia
Loffredo (Zoë)

The Jones Group
342 Marietta St., Suite #3
Atlanta, GA 30313
USA
404-523-2606
www.thejonesgroup.com

0194, 0230
Art Director: Vicky Jones
Designer: Kendra Lively
Client: Cenitare Restaurant Group

0200
Art Director: Vicky Jones
Designer: Brody Boyer
Client: Old Edwards Hospitality
Group

0229
Art Director: Vicky Jones
Designer: Chris Lowndes
Client: Cenitare Restaurant Group

0287
Art Director: Vicky Jones
Designer: Kendra Lively
Client: Cenitare Restaurant Group

0325
Art Director: Vicky Jones
Designer: Kendra Lively
Client: Old Edwards Hospitality
Group

0326
Art Director: Vicky Jones
Designer: Chris Lowndes
Client: Cenitare Restaurant Group

0388
Art Director: Vicky Jones
Designer: Kendra Lively
Client: Fotos Group

Jonni
Markreien 33b
0554 Oslo
Norway
+47 905 18 186
www.bleed.no

**0088, 0090, 0106, 0183, 0421,
0424**
Art Director: Jonni
Designer: Jonni
Client: Café Kaos

Kapp & Associates, Inc.
2729 Prospect Ave.
Cleveland, OH 44115
USA

0563
Art Director: Cathryn Kapp
Designers: Derek Oyen, Sally Biel
Client: Sammy's at the Arena

Kenneth Diseño
Miguel Treviño s/n Fabrica San
Pedro, Centro
Uruapan Michoacan 60000
Mexico
+52 452 523 1738
mail@kengraf.net

0089
Art Director: Kenneth Treviño
Designers: Kenneth Treviño,
Minerva Galván
Client: Sunset

0127, 0367
Art Director: Kenneth Treviño
Designer: Kenneth Treviño
Client: La Placita

0145, 0351
Art Director: Kenneth Treviño
Designers: Kenneth Treviño,
Minerva Galván
Client: Café La Pérgola

0146, 0370
Art Director: Kenneth Treviño
Designer: Kenneth Treviño
Client: Dennis Pizza

0197
Art Director: Kenneth Treviño
Designers: Kenneth Treviño,
Sheila Peña R.
Client: Miura Bar

0199
Art Director: Kenneth Treviño
Designer: Kenneth Treviño
Client: Texas BBQ

0310
Art Director: Kenneth Treviño
Designer: Kenneth Treviño
Client: La Fontana

0363
Art Director: Kenneth Treviño
Designer: Kenneth Treviño
Client: La Lupita

0364
Art Director: Kenneth Treviño
Designer: Kenneth Treviño
Client: Mr. Costillas

0365
Art Director: Kenneth Treviño
Designers: Kenneth Treviño,
Minerva Galván
Client: Aqui Nomas

0366
Art Director: Kenneth Treviño
Designer: Kenneth Treviño
Client: Hippos

0368
Art Director: Kenneth Treviño
Designer: Kenneth Treviño
Client: Pollo Carretas

0369
Art Director: Kenneth Treviño
Designer: Kenneth Treviño
Client: El Tope

**Laguna College of Art &
Design**
2222 Laguna Canyon Rd.
Laguna Beach, CA 92651
Mailing address: 10 Thunder Run,
6-d
Irvine, CA 92614
USA
949-551-5662
www.lagunacollege.edu
atiragram3@hotmail.com

Lorenza Zanni
Via Avanzini 17
41100 Modena
Italy
+39 059 2928012
doppiazeta@libero.it

0279
Art Director: Lorenza Zanni
Designer: Lorenza Zanni
Client: Shibuya

Louise Fili Ltd.
71 Fifth Ave.
New York, NY 10003
USA

0742
Designer: Louise Fili
Client: Espace

Mark Frankel Design, Inc
479 Newport Dr.
Naperville, IL 60565
USA
630-717-7630
www.markfrankeldesign.com

0282, 0319, 0328, 0431, 0433,
0438
Art Director: Kirsten Mentley
Designer: Mark Frankel
Client: Levy Restaurants

Marve Cooper Design, Ltd.
2120 W. Grand
Chicago, IL 60612
USA

0163, 0667
Art Director: Marve Cooper
Designers: Keith Curtis,
Marve Cooper
Client: Tapas Barcelona
(Restaurant Development Group)

Mary Hutchison Design LLC
4010 Whitman Ave. N
Seattle, WA 98103
USA
206-407-3460
www.maryhutchisondesign.com
info@maryhutchisondesign.com

0129, 0267, 0578, 0999
Art Director: Mary Chin Hutchison
Designer: Mary Chin Hutchison
Client: O'Asian Bistro, Inc.

McCord Graphic Design
Contact information not available

0487
Art Director: Walter McCord
Designer: Walter McCord
Illustrators: Charles Loupot,
Bud Hixson
Clients: Joanne Deitrich,
Bim Deitrich (Deitrich's in the
Cresent)

0662
Art Director: Walter McCord
Designer: Walter McCord
Illustrator: Walter McCord
Clients: Kathy Cary,
Will Cary (Lilly's)

The Menu Workshop
2815 Second Ave. #393
Seattle, WA 98121
USA
206-443-9516

0432
Art Director: Liz Kearney
Designer: Liz Kearney
Illustrator: Debbie Hanley
Client: J.J. Fryes

Milton Glaser, Inc
207 East 32nd St.
New York, NY 10016
USA
212-889-3161
www.miltonglaser.com
studio@miltonglaser.com

0027, 0028, 0029, 0030
Client: Stony Brook University

Mimolimit
Studio Najbrt
Fráni Šrámka 15
Praha 5
150 00 Czech Republic
+420 257 561060
www.najbrt.cz
studio@najbrt.cz

0026, 0108, 0109, 0483, 0484,
0485, 0486
Art Director: Aleš Najbrt
Designer: Bohumil Vašák
Client: Saxo Consulting

0158, 0436, 0766, 0767
Art Director: Aleš Najbrt
Designer: Aleš Najbrt
Client: DJ Svět, SVO

0178, 0437, 0724
Art Director: Aleš Najbrt
Designer: Zuzana Ledhická
Client: Targa Consulting

Mind's Eye Studio
PO Box 194
East Kelowna, BC V0H 1G0
Canada

0652, 0654
Art Director: Valery Mercer
Designer: Valery Mercer
Illustrator: Michael Downs
Client: Bailly's

Minelli, Inc
381 Congress St.
Boston, MA 02210
USA
617-426-5343
www.minelli.com
webmail@minelli.com

0111, 0112, 0378, 0400
Art Director: Margarita Barrios
Ponce
Designer: Stephen Rowe
Creative Director:
Client: Oxford Street Grill

Mirko Ilić Corp.
207 East 32nd St.
New York, NY 10016
USA
212-481-9737
www.mirkoilic.com
studio@mirkoilic.com

0130, 0131, 0132, 0416, 0542,
0737, 0754, 0755, 0756, 0757,
0759, 0760, 0761, 0762, 0763,
0972
Art Director: Mirko Ilić
Designers: Mirko Ilić, Clint Shaner
Client: Le Cirque

0730, 0758, 0765, 0983
Art Director: Mirko Ilić
Designers: Mirko Ilić, Clint Shaner
Client: Summit

Mixer
Löwenplatz 5
CH-6004 Lucerne
Switzerland
+41 41 410 35 35
www.mixer.ch

0387, 0590, 0842
Art Director: Erich Brechbühl
Designer: Erich Brechbühl
Client: Wirtschaft zur Schlacht

Morrow McKenzie Design
322 NW 5th Ave., Suite 313
Portland, OR 97209
USA
503-222-0331
www.morrowmckenzie.com

0206, 0428
Art Director: Elizabeth Morrow
McKenzie
Designer: Elizabeth Morrow
McKenzie
Client: Carafe Restaurant

Nita B. Creative
991 Selby Ave.
St. Paul, MN 55104
USA
651-644-2889
www.nitabcreative.com

0771
Art Director: Renita Breitenbucher
Designer: Renita Breitenbucher
Client: Thirst

Northern Artisan
PO Box 187
Rockwood, ME 04478
USA
207-534-2287

0849
Art Director: Jane Perry
Designer: Greg Donnelly
Client: Roadkill Café

Octavo Design Pty Ltd
11 Yarra St.
South Melbourne, Victoria, 3205
Australia
+613 9686 4703
www.octavodesign.com.au
info@octavodesign.com.au

0239, 0482, 0974
Art Director: Gary Domoney
Designer: Gary Domoney
Client: Da Vinci's

0300, 0478, 0975
Art Director: Gary Domoney
Designer: Gary Domoney
Client: Indulge

0301, 0976
Art Director: Gary Domoney
Designer: Gary Domoney
Client: Verve

0323, 0832, 0967
Art Director: Gary Domoney
Designer: Gary Domoney
Client: Kanela

Oliver Russell
217 South 11th St.
Boise, ID 83702
USA
208-287-6528
www.oliverrussell.com

0290
Art Directors: Tony Robin,
Paul Carew
Designer: Tony Robin
Client: Franco Latino Restaurant

0330
Art Director: Paul Carew
Designer: Colleen Cahill
Client: Mortimer's Restaurant

On the Edge Design, Inc
1601 Dove St., #294
Newport Beach, CA 92660
USA
949-251-0025
www.ontheedgedesign.com
info@ontheedgedesign.com

0371, 0924, 0925, 0926, 0955
Art Director: Gina Mims
Designers: Charissa Armenta,
Leny Evangelista
Client: The Lost Bean Organic
Coffee & Tea

0552, 0985
Art Directors: Gina Mims,
Jeff Gasper
Designer: Melanie Fujita
Client: Honolulu Harry's Island
Getaway

0553, 0987
Art Directors: Gina Mims,
Jeff Gasper
Designer: Melanie Fujita
Client: The Lazy Dog Café

0595, 0775, 0797, 0798, 0984
Art Directors: Gina Mims,
Jeff Gasper
Designer: Melanie Fujita
Client: Sutra Lounge

0650
Art Director: Joe Mozdzen
Designer: Jeff Gasper
Client: The Rex

0779, 0780, 0800, 0986
Art Director: Jeff Gasper
Designer: Tracey Lamberson
Client: Chat Noir Bistro & Jazz
Lounge

**0879, 0880, 0881, 0893, 0894,
0895**
Art Director: Gina Mims
Designer: Gina Mims
Client: Yogurt Mill

Pentagram Design
204 Fifth Ave.
New York, NY 10010
USA

0072, 0092, 0620, 0621, 0743
Art Director: Michael Bierut
Designers: Michael Bierut,
Lisa Cerveny
Illustrator: Woody Pirtle
Photographer: Reven TC Wurman

Client: Gotham Equities (The
Good Diner)

0091, 0172
Art Directors: Michael Bierut
(graphics), James Biber (interiors)
Designer: Emily Hayes
Photographer: Peter Mauss/Esto
Client: Route 66 Roadhouse &
Dining Saloon (George Korten,
Martin Winkler, Kent Selig)

0550
Art Directors: Paula Scher
(graphics), James Biber (interiors)
Designer: Ron Louie
Photographer: Peter Mauss/Esto
Client: One Fifth Avenue (Jérome
Kretchmer)

Ph.D
1524A Cloverfield Blvd.
Santa Monica, CA 90404
USA
310-829-0900
www.phdla.com

0226
Art Directors: Michael Hodgson,
Clive Piercy
Designer: Michael Hodgson
Client: Bergamot Café

PM Design
11 Maple Terrace
Verona, NJ 07044
USA

0639
Art Director: Philip Marzo
Designer: Philip Marzo
Photographer: Geoff Reed
Client: Marion Scotto

Poulin & Morris
286 Spring St., Sixth Floor
New York, NY 10013
USA
212-675-1332
www.poulinmorris.com
info@poulinmorris.com

0093, 0399, 0977
Designers: Richard Poulin, Brian
Brindisi, Anna Crider
Client: Dahesh Museum of Art

PPA Design Limited
11 Macdonnell Rd. D-3
Midlevels
Hong Kong

0610, 0611
Art Director: Byron Jacobs
Designers: Byron Jacobs,
Bernard Cau
Client: Cathay Pacific Airways

0628
Art Director: Byron Jacobs
Designers: Byron Jacobs,
Don Funk
Illustrator: Brian Grimwood
Client: Dragon Airlines

0640, 0668, 0669
Art Director: Byron Jacobs
Designers: Byron Jacobs, Tracy Hoi
Photographer: Ka Sing Lee
Client: Cathay Pacific Airways

Prejean Creative
305 La Rue France, Suite 200
Lafayette, LA 70508
USA
337-593-9051
www.prejeancreative.com

0245
Art Director: Kevin Prejean
Designer: Kevin Prejean
Client: Lafayette Convention and
Visitors Commission

0246
Art Directors: Kevin Prejean,
Gary LoBue
Designers: Mindi Nash,
Kevin Prejean
Client: Evangeline Downs
Racetrack & Casino

0248
Art Directors: Kevin Prejean,
Gary LoBue
Designer: Gary LoBue
Client: Evangeline Downs
Racetrack & Casino

0292, 0604, 0605, 0606, 0607
Art Directors: Kevin Prejean,
Gary LoBue
Designer: Kevin Prejean
Client: Evangeline Downs
Racetrack & Casino

Public:
10 Arkansas, Suite L
San Francisco, CA 94107
USA
415-863-2541
www.publicdesign.com

**0458, 0460, 0932, 0933, 0934,
0935, 0936, 0938**
Art Director: Todd Foreman
Designers: Todd Foreman,
Tessa Lee, Nancy Thomas,
Lindsay Wheeler
Client: Café Lo Cubano

**0459, 0461, 0462, 0783, 0784,
0903**
Art Director: Todd Foreman
Designer: Lindsay Wheeler
Client: Straits Restaurant

**0463, 0464, 0465, 0530, 0740,
0904**
Art Director: Todd Foreman
Designers: Todd Foreman,
Tessa Lee, Nancy Thomas,
Lindsay Wheeler
Client: Bistro Vida

0466, 0467, 0470, 0684
Art Director: Todd Foreman
Designers: Todd Foreman,
Tessa Lee, Nancy Thomas,
Lindsay Wheeler
Client: Sino

Q
Sonnenberger Str. 16
Wiesbaden 65193
Germany
+49 611 181.31.0
info@a-home.de

0076, 0077, 0234
Art Director: Matthias Frey
Designer: Matthias Frey
Client: Blattgold Bar & Restaurant,
Hanover

0228
Art Director: Laurenz Nielbock
Client: Stiller's

0283
Art Director: Laurenz Nielbock
Client: L'Auberge

Qually & Company
2238 East Central St.
Evanston, IL 60201
USA
708-864-6316

0160
Art Director: Robert Qually
Designers: Robert Qually, Holly
Thomas, Karla Walusiaki,
Charles Sonties
Client: Windy City Café

R&Mag Graphic Design
Via del Pescatore 3
80053 Castellammare di Stabia
Italy
+39 081 8705053
www.remag.it
info@remag.it

0044, 0142, 0334
Art Director: Fontanella, Di Somma,
Cesar
Designer: Fontanella, Di Somma,
Cesar
Client: Sapori D'Italia

0074, 0217, 0584
Art Director: Fontanella, Di Somma,
Cesar
Designer: Fontanella, Di Somma,
Cesar
Client: Puldí

0133, 0829
Art Director: Fontanella, Di Somma,
Cesar
Designer: Fontanella, Di Somma,
Cesar
Client: Sunshine

0140, 0377, 0518
Art Director: Fontanella, Di Somma,
Cesar
Designer: Fontanella, Di Somma,
Cesar
Client: Le Terrazze

0143, 0270, 0683, 0811
Art Director: Fontanella, Di Somma,
Cesar
Designer: Fontanella, Di Somma,
Cesar
Client: The Wine Bar

0348, 0819
Art Director: Fontanella, Di Somma,
Cesar
Designer: Fontanella, Di Somma,
Cesar
Client: Bar Di Martino

0586
Art Director: Fontanella, Di Somma,
Cesar
Designer: Fontanella, Di Somma,
Cesar
Client: Vittó Pizza

Raidy Printing Group SAL
Postal Code 2071 3203
PO Box 175 165
Beirut
Lebanon
+961 1 56 7711
Mobile +961 323 4411
www.raidy.com
design@raidy.com

0232, 0656, 0739
Art Director: Marie-Joe J. Raidy
Designer: Marie-Joe J. Raidy
Client: Chantal Braidi

Raven Madd Design Company
PO Box 11.331 Wellington
Level 3 Harcourts Building
Corner Grey St. and Lambton Quay
New Zealand

0612
Art Director: Mark Curtis
Designer: Mark Curtis
Illustrators: Mark Curtis,
Caroline Campbell
Client: Chevy's (John Wiley)

Regan Blough
2112 W North Ave., Apt. 2W
Chicago, IL 60647
USA
773-227-3690
reganblough@sbcglobal.net

0320, 0718, 0736
Designer: Regan Blough
Client: The Smoke Daddy

0386, 0992
Art Director: Jilly Simons
Designer: Regan Todd
Client: D.O.C. Wine Bar

Re-Public
Laplandsgade 4
2300 Copenhagen S
Denmark
+45 4095 5180
www.re-public.com
emil@re-public.com

0227, 0820
Art Director: Emil Hartvig
Designer: Emil Hartvig
Client: Hacienda

Restaurant Identity.com
62 Robbins Ave.
Berkeley Heights, NJ 07922
USA
903-665-6878

0266
Art Director: Philip Marzo
Designers: Philip Marzo,
DeeDee Burnside
Client: Sara Chea

0361
Art Director: Philip Marzo
Designers: Philip Marzo,
Andrei Koribanics
Client: A. Rodriguez

0362
Art Director: Philip Marzo
Designers: Philip Marzo, Dave Sailer
Client: Glenn Susser

0389
Art Director: Philip Marzo
Designer: Philip Marzo
Client: Harvest Restaurants

0544
Art Director: Philip Marzo
Designer: Philip Marzo
Client: Village Cellar

Richard Poulin Design Group
286 Spring St.
6th Floor
New York, NY 10013
USA
212-929-5445

0068
Art Director: Richard Poulin
Designer: Richard Poulin
Client: Merchandise Mart
Properties, Inc.

0638
Art Director: Richard Poulin
Designer: Richard Poulin
Client: United Nations Plaza Hotel
(Ambassador Grill)

0648
Art Director: Richard Poulin
Designer: Richard Poulin
Client: The Drake Hotel, New York
City (La Piazzetta)

Rickabaugh Graphics
384 West Johnstown Rd.
Gahanna, OH 43230
USA
614-337-2229

0395
Art Director: Barry Spector
Designer: Barry Spector
Illustrator: Suzanne Ketchoyian
Client: Grace Restaurant Services
(Broadway Museum Café)

0435
Art Director: Eric Rickabaugh
Designer: Tina Zientarski
Illustrator: Tina Zientarski
Client: Fritz & Alfredo's

Rome & Gold Creative
1606 Central Ave. SE, Suite 102
Albuquerque, NM 87106
USA
505-897-0870
www.rgcreative.com

**0017, 0018, 0019, 0022, 0023,
0024**
Art Director: Lorenzo Romero
Designer: Robert E. Goldie
Client: Boba Tea Company

0021
Art Director: Robert E. Goldie
Designer: Lorenzo Romero
Client: Solomon's Porch

0295
Art Director: John Sayles
Designer: John Sayles
Client: Sauce

0633
Art Director: John Sayles
Designer: Bill Nellans
Client: Chelsea Restaurant and Bar
(Westin Chicago)

0649
Art Director: John Sayles
Designer: Bill Nellans
Client: 801 Steak & Chop House

Schumaker
466 Green
San Francisco, CA 94133
USA
415-398-1060

0635
Art Director: Ward Schumaker
Designer: Ward Schumaker
Client: Moose's

Sea Design
70 St. John St.
London EC1M 4DT
UK
+44 020 7566 3100
www.seadesign.co.uk

**0001, 0002, 0003, 0078, 0107,
0179**
Art Directors: John Simpson,
Bryan Edmondson
Client: OQO

Shamlian Advertising
128 Mansion Dr.
Media, PA 19063
USA

0665
Art Director: Fred Shamlian
Designer: Stephen Bagi
Illustrators: Heidi Stevens, Susan
Harvey, Ginger DiMaio
Photographers: Barry Halkin,
Joe Farley
Client: Passerelle

sky design
50 Hurt Plaza, Suite 500
Atlanta, GA 30303
USA
404-688-4702
tvaught@at.asdnet.com

0041, 0042, 0126, 0906
Art Director: Thom Williams
Designer: W. Todd Vaught
Client: Toast

0134, 0135, 0698, 0699, 0729
Art Director: W. Todd Vaught
Designers: W. Todd Vaught, Carrie
Brown, Tiffany Chen
Client: Concentrics Restaurant
Group

Smart Works
113 Ferrars St.
Southbank, Victoria 3006
Australia
+61 03 8699 1111
www.smartworks.com.au

0258, 0600, 0833, 0869, 0911
Art Director: Paul Smith
Designer: Paul Smith
Client: Funk Fish Café

Spark Communications Inc
327 E Maryland Ave.
Royal Oak, MI 48067
USA
248-545-9012
www.spark-communications.com

0304
Art Director: Sherri Lawton
Designer: Sherri Lawton
Client: The Inn Place

Spark Studio Pty Ltd
11 Yarra St.
South Melbourne, Victoria, 3205
Australia
+613 9686 4703
www.sparkstudio.com.au
info@sparkstudio.com.au

0223, 0422, 0858, 0913
Art Director: Sean Pethick
Designer: Natalie Leys
Client: Three Below

Stanley Moscowitz Graphics
474 Upper Samsonville Rd.
Samsonville, NY 12476
USA
914-657-8974

0314
Art Director: Stanley Moscowitz
Designer: Stanley Moscowitz
Illustrator: Stanley Moscowitz
Client: On Rye

Strata-Media Inc
3590 Harbor Gateway N
Costa Mesa, CA 92626
USA
714-460-1205
www.strata-media.com

0214
Art Director: Todd Henderson
Designers: Todd Henderson,
Jason Simon
Client: Creme de la Creme

STRONGtype
91 Prospect St.
Dover, NJ 07802-1520
USA
973-919-4265
www.strongtype.com

0415
Art Director: Richard Puder
Client: Faregrounds Restaurant

Studio Output

2 Broadway
The Lace Market
NG1 1PS Nottingham
UK
+44 0 115 950 7116
www.studio-output.com
info@studio-output.com

0006, 0007, 0177, 0439, 0440
Designer: Rob Cole
Client: Tea Factory

0008, 0009, 0010, 0039, 0189
Art Director: Dan Moore
Designer: Lydia Lapinski
Client: Geisha

0083, 0084, 0175
Art Director: Steve Payne
Designer: Steve Payne
Client: Brass Monkey

0176, 0411
Art Director: Dan Moore
Designer: Sara Oakley
Photographer: Philip Watts
Client: Lizard Lounge

Studio Siereeni

708 South Orange Grove
Los Angeles, CA 90036
USA
213-937-0355

0257
Art Directors: Richard Seireeni,
Romane Cameron
Designer: Romane Cameron
Illustrator: Romane Cameron
Client: Fred's 62

Taxi Studio Ltd

93 Princess Victoria St.
Clifton, Bristol BS8 4DD
UK
+44 0 117 973 5151
www.taxistudio.co.uk

0102, 0104, 0233, 0401
Art Director: Spencer Buck
Designer: Olly Guise
Client: Goldbrick House

TD2, Identity & Strategic Design

Ibsen 43, 8th Floor. Polanco
México D.F. 11560
Mexico
+52 55 5281 6999
www.td2.com.mx
contacto@td2.com.mx

0202
Art Director: Rafael Treviño
Designers: Rodrigo Córdova,
Adalberto Arenas, Mauricio Muñoz
Client: La Posada

0305
Art Directors: Rafael Treviño,
Rodrigo Córdova
Designer: José Luis Patiño
Client: Frankfurt Restaurant

0339
Art Director: Rodrigo Córdova
Designer: Rodrigo Córdova
Client: Sutra

0340
Art Director: Rafael Treviño
Designers: Rodrigo Córdova,
Gabriela Zamora
Client: Yushan Restaurant

0341
Art Director: Rafael Treviño
Designers: Rodrigo Córdova,
Mauricio Muñoz
Client: Chin-ai

0753
Art Director: Rafael Treviño
Designers: Gabriela Zamora,
Rodrigo Córdova
Client: Paddock Café

Tharp Did It

50 University Ave.
Suite 21
Los Gatos, CA 95030
USA
408-354-6726

0139
Art Director: Rick Tharp
Designers: Rick Tharp, Jean
Mogannam, Jana Heer
Client: Le Boulanger Bakeries

0164
Art Director: Rick Tharp
Designers: Rick Tharp,
Jean Mogannam
Client: Bakeries by the Bay
(101 Bakery Café)

The Art Commission, Inc.

2287 Capehart Cr. NE
Atlanta, GA 30345
USA
404-636-9149

0169
Art Director: Bruce Phillips
Designer: Cynthia Virkler
Illustrators: Bruce Phillips,
Cynthia Virkler
Client: Shelia Thacker (Thames
Street Tavern)

The Invisions Group Ltd.

4927 Auburn Ave.
Suite 100
Bethesda, MD 20814-2641
USA

0173, 0392
Art Director: John Cabot Lodge
Designers: Denise Sparhawk,
Michael Kraine
Client: Kinkead's (Robert Kinkead)

Thielen Designs
115 Gold Ave., Suite 209
Albuquerque, NM 87104
USA
505-205-3157
www.thielendesigns.com

0313, 0322
Art Director: Tony Thielen
Designer: Tony Thielen
Client: Sunshine Café

0321
Art Director: Tony Thielen
Designers: Tony Thielen, Randy Heil
Client: Sunshine Café

Threefold
95 Green St.
Richmond
Melbourne, VIC 3121
Australia
+61 3 9421 8988
belinda@threefold.com.au

0298, 0441, 0716, 0857, 0861,
0921
Art Director: Pom Kimber
Designer: Pom Kimber
Illustrator: Tom Samek
Client: Vue de Monde

Tomato Košir
Britop 141
S1-4000 Kranj
Slovenia
+386 41 260 979
tomato@siol.net

0151
Art Director: Tomato Košir
Designer: Tomato Košir
Client: Sax Pub

Tom Varisco Designs
608 Baronne St.
New Orleans, LA 70113
USA
514-410-2888
www.tomvariscodesigns.com

0196
Art Director: Tom Varisco
Designers: Rebecca Carr, Jeff
Louviere, David Caruso
Client: Cochon

Turnstyle
2219 NW Market St.
Seattle, WA 98107
USA
206-297-7350
www.turnstylestudio.com

0195, 0746, 0824, 0917
Art Director: Ben Graham
Designers: Ben Graham,
Steve Watson
Client: Matador Restaurant

Ultra Design
2454, Rua Padre
Anchieta
Curitiba PR 80730 000
Brazil
+55 (41) 3016 3023
www.ultradesign.com.br

0240, 0593, 0776
Art Director: Braulio Carollo
Designer: Raul Ramos
Client: Roy Bean Burgers

0353, 0613
Art Director: Braulio Carollo
Designer: Raul Ramos
Client: Villa Marcolini

0354
Art Director: Braulio Carollo
Designer: Braulio Carollo
Client: Marcolini Gelateria

Unreal
12 Dyott St.
London WC1A 1DE
UK
+44 0 20 7379 8752
www.unreal-uk.com

0181
Art Director: Brian Eagle
Designer: Copper Giles
Client: Sphere

0182
Art Director: Brian Eagle
Designer: Copper Giles
Client: Shake

0184
Art Director: Brian Eagle
Designer: M. R. Bragg
Client: Food Food

0383
Art Director: M. R. Bragg
Client: The Cock & Trumpet

urban INFLUENCE Design Studio
423 Second Ave. Ext., South
Suite 32
Seattle, WA 98104
USA
206-219-5599 x204
www.urbaninfluence.com

0161, 0190, 0715
Art Director: Henry Yiu
Designer: Mike Mates
Client: Ticklefish

0191, 0929, 0930
Art Director: Henry Yiu
Designers: Mike Mates, Pete
Wright, Henry Yiu
Client: La Vita E Bella

0409
Art Director: Henry Yiu
Designers: Henry Yiu (folder),
Ivona Konarski, Mike Mates,
Henry Yiu (inside pages only)
Client: Queen City Grill

0410
Art Director: Henry Yiu
Designers: Henry Yiu (folder), Ivona
Konarski, Mike Mates, Henry Yiu
(inside pages only)
Client: Frontier Room

Val Gene Associates
5208 Classen Blvd.
Oklahoma City, OK 73118
USA

0488, 0564, 0565, 0566
Art Director: Lacy Leverett
Designer: Lacy Leverett
Photographer: Chuck Doswell III
Production: Shirley Morrow
Client: Eagle's Nest

0579, 0580
Art Director: Lacy Leverett
Designer: Lacy Leverett
Illustrators: Morrow Design,
Shirley Morrow
Client: Harry's American Grill & Bar

0581
Art Director: Lacy Leverett
Client: Pepperoni Grill

0601
Art Director: Lacy Leverett
Designer: Lacy Leverett
Illustrator: Christopher Jennings
Production: Shirley Morrow
Client: Shorty Small's Great
American Restaurant

VINE360
9851 Harrison Rd. #320
Bloomington, MN 55437
USA
952-893-0504
www.VINE360.com
info@VINE360.com

0250
Designer: Joy Mac Donald
Client: Bittersweet

Vital Signs & Graphics
10 Timber Ln.
Ellington, CT 06029
USA
203-875-9745

0085, 0086, 0170
Art Director: Denise Fopiano
Benoit
Designer: Denise Fopiano Benoit
Client: W.B. Cody's Bar-B-Que
Grille

Vrontikis Design Office
2707 Westwood Blvd.
Los Angeles, CA 90064
USA
310-446-5446
www.35k.com

0114, 0121, 0122, 0231
Art Director: Petrula Vrontikis
Designer: Petrula Vrontikis
Client: Global Dining, Inc.

0275, 0744, 0781, 0794
Art Director: Petrula Vrontikis
Designer: Petrula Vrontikis
Client: Global Dining, Inc.

0331, 0710, 0728, 0990
Art Director: Petrula Vrontikis
Designers: Petrula Vrontikis, Lorna
Stovall (logo lettering), Trina Luong,
Deanna Thagard, Reagan Marshall
Client: Calistoga Bakery Café

0347, 0870
Art Director: Petrula Vrontikis
Designer: Katsu Nakamachi
Client: Global Dining, Inc.

0350
Art Director: Petrula Vrontikis
Designers: Petrula Vrontikis,
May Hartono
Client: Global Dining, Inc.

0374, 0825
Art Director: Petrula Vrontikis
Designer: Christina Hsaio
Client: Global Dining, Inc.

0655
Art Director: Petrula Vrontikis
Designer: Kim Sage
Client: Jacksons (Alan Jackson)

Walker Group
95 Morton St., 8th Floor
New York, NY 10014
USA
212-462-8000
www.wgcni.com

0056, 0071
Art Director: George Kewin
Designers: Ana Luisa Rolim, Brian
Cuba, Rob Lopez
Client: Pauli Moto's Asian Bistro

Warm Rain Ltd
67 Vyner St.
London E2 9DQ
UK
+44 020 8980 1984
www.warmrain.co.uk
studio@warmrain.co.uk

**0069, 0691, 0692, 0693, 0694,
0733, 0786, 0801, 0931**
Art Director: Mark Lawson Bell
Designer: Warm Rain Design Team
Client: Sketch

0280, 0864, 0865
Art Director: Mark Lawson Bell
Designer: Warm Rain Design Team
Client: Imli

0591, 0592, 0678, 0679, 0989
Art Director: Mark Lawson Bell
Designer: Warm Rain Design Team
Client: Sketch

0843, 0844, 0845, 0846
Art Director: Mark Lawson Bell
Designer: Murray Thompson
Client: Sketch

0847
Art Director: Mark Lawson Bell
Designers: Murray Thompson,
Eva Simon
Client: Sketch

0848
Art Director: Mark Lawson Bell
Designers: Murray Thompson,
Jonathan Stuart
Client: Sketch

0851
Art Director: Mark Lawson Bell
Designers: Nina Zeigler, Jurgen Bey
Client: Sketch

Whitney-Edwards Design
14 West Dover St.
PO Box 2425
Easton, MD 21601
USA

0616
Art Director: Charlene Whitney-
Edwards
Designer: Barbi Christopher
Illustrator: Charlene Whitney-
Edwards
Client: Washington Street Pub

Willoughby Design Group
602 Westport Rd.
Kansas City, MO 64111
USA
816-561-4189
www.willoughbydesign.com

**0011, 0012, 0015, 0025, 0549,
0695**
Art Directors: Ann Willoughby,
Zack Shubkagel
Designers: Stephanie Lee, Brady
Vest (Hammerpress)
Client: SPIN! Concepts (Gail Lozoff)

**0013, 0014, 0016, 0547, 0706,
0816, 0817, 0968, 0969**
Art Directors: Ann Willoughby,
Zack Shubkagel
Designers: Nate Hardin,
Jessica McEntire
Client: Sheridan's Lattés,
Frozen Custard

Wolken Communica
2562 Dexter Ave. N
Seattle, WA 98109
USA
206-545-1696
www.wolkencommunica.com

0237
Art Director: Kurt Wolken
Designers: Johann Gómez,
Ryan Burlinson
Client: Wonder Bar

XJR Design
700 N. Green St.
Chicago, IL 60622
USA
312-243-3377

0641
Art Director: Roger Foin
Designers: Roger Foin, Wilda Kemp
Illustrator: Leonardo da Vinci, with
alterations by the designers
Client: Paul LoDuca, Kathy LoDuca
(Vinci)

⋯➤

ABOUT THE AUTHOR

Luke Herriott runs a UK-based design group called **Studio Ink,** specializing in design for print. As former design director of the international visual arts publisher Rotovision, he has worked with some of the world's leading creatives to produce a number of outstanding design publications.

With more than 15 years in the book publishing industry, he has a wealth of experience and an extensive knowledge of design, as well as a good awareness and appreciation of emerging graphic trends.

He is author of Rotovision's **The Packaging and Design Templates Sourcebook** and **The Designer's Packaging Bible** and co-author of **First Steps in Digital Design** and **Instant Graphics.**